LIVING DHARMA

Dzalendara Publishing
Rokpa Trust
Kagyu Samye Ling Monastery and Tibetan Centre
Eskdalemuir Dumfriesshire DG13 0QL
Scotland UK
www.samye.org

Front cover photograph by Pasi Haaranen.
Back cover photograph by Richard Baker

> *Proceeds from the sale of this book will be divided between the Samye Sangha Foundation, which helps to support the monks and nuns of Samye Ling in their spiritual endeavours, and the rebuilding of Choje Akong Tulku Rinpoche's monastery of Dolma Lhakang in East Tibet.*

Namo

I pay homage to the Buddha, Dharma and Sangha, and to my root Guru, His Holiness the 16th Gyalwa Karmapa, Rangjung Rikpe Dorje and his reincarnation, His Holiness the 17th Gyalwa Karmapa, Urgyen Trinley Dorje.

I pray that this humble book of mine will bring great benefit to all beings. It is dedicated to my brother, Choje Akong Tulku Rinpoche, to whom I owe everything.

His Holiness the 17th Gyalwa Karmapa Urgen Trinley Dorje

Khentin Tai Situpa   Goshir Gyaltsapa

Choje Akong Tulku Rinpoche

Photo John Cunniff

Lama Yeshe Losal and Choje Akong Tulku Rinpoche

v

Ven Lama Yeshe Losal
Chairman of Rokpa Trust
Abbot and Retreat Master
of Samye Ling

Eskdalemuir, Langholm
Dumfriesshire, DG13 0QL
Scotland, UK
web: www.samyeling.org

Karma Drubgyud Darjay Ling Monastery

Foreword and Acknowledgements

A year ago I had no intention of ever writing a book. I was simply doing what I feel I do best, that is meditating and working to help establish the Dharma in the West. Then last year I was invited to Germany and Belgium to lead several meditation courses. And in April of this year, just after finishing three months' intensive retreat, I was asked to give a weekend course in London.

My students in Germany, Belgium and London transcribed these courses from tapes and tried hard to persuade me that the transcripts were worthy of printing in book form. The resulting book is not based on my academic understanding of Buddhist philosophy, but is the fruit of many years' experience of sincere meditation. It springs from the understanding I have gained through the practice of meditation and deals with the practical application of the Buddhist teachings to everyday life.

If you are interested in Buddhism or you are already a practitioner, and find it useful for your Dharma practice, may I offer this little book as food for your spiritual growth. If on the other hand, your interest is more intellectual and my book is not scholarly enough then I humbly ask forgiveness.

This book could not have come about without the hard work and dedication of many of my students. I would like to thank in particular Corinne Segers from Brussels for all her work in merging the transcripts from the many talks into one. Without her commitment, it would have been impossible to bring this book to completion so quickly. Many of my Sangha also worked very hard on the transcript to polish it into its present form. I would sincerely like to thank them for all their efforts.

However, during the whole process I always kept in mind the example of the golden statue. If we polish it too much, the gold wears away. Consequently I have made sure that, at every stage of its evolution, the text of the book retained my original meaning, even though my broken English may have been mended.

As I didn't know that my teachings would ever become a book, my words are very simple and direct. I hope you find something useful in them. If you disagree with anything, or find it hurtful, please remember this is only my view of things - I don't expect everyone to agree with what I say!

I pray that this little book will make a small contribution towards firmly establishing the jewel of the Dharma in the West - and thereby benefit all sentient beings.

Ven. Lama Yeshe Losal
Kagyu Samye Ling Monastery
6th June, 2001

CONTENTS

ABOUT THE AUTHOR

Venerable Lama Yeshe Losal is the colourful and charismatic Abbot of Kagyu Samye Ling Monastery and Tibetan Centre, Director of the internationally acclaimed Holy Island Project and the much loved and respected Retreat and Meditation Master for a host of students from around the world. This book, based on transcripts from some of Lama Yeshe Losal's recent teachings, was compiled by a dedicated team of those students, who worked together with the common aim of sharing the wisdom and wit of their teacher with a wider audience.

The main body of the book deals with the practical application of Buddhism in one's daily life. In his direct, down to earth style, Lama Yeshe Losal both demystifies and illuminates these profound teachings in such a way as to make them easily understood and accessible to even the most obdurate mind. With his insight, humour, and knowledge of a broad spectrum of people from both the East and the West, Lama Yeshe teaches from the Buddhist perspective on life and gives practical advice, with detailed meditation instructions, in a simple but inspiring way. Before embarking on the teachings that follow, readers may find it of interest to know some of his biographical details in order to get a flavour of this remarkable man and his fascinating life.

Born in 1943 to a farming family in Kham, east Tibet and named Jamphel Drakpa, or Jamdrak for short, he spent an idyllic early childhood close to nature, helping his family with the yaks and sheep and playing in the lush pastures with other village children. This carefree existence came to an abrupt end when young Jamdrak was chosen to join his brother, Choje Akong Tulku Rinpoche at his monastery of Dolma Lhakang. Akong Tulku Rinpoche's birth had been accompanied by many auspicious signs and, although he was only three years older than Jamdrak, he had been recognised as a Tulku, or reincarnate Lama, by the then head of the Kagyu Lineage, His Holiness the 16th Karmapa. At the age of six he had been enthroned as Abbot of Dolma Lhakang monastery where he began rigorous training in the teachings of Tibetan Buddhism.

It is a Tibetan tradition that if a Tulku is head of a monastery, then one of his brothers is trained to assist him. As many auspicious signs had also occurred when Jamdrak was born and he too had been recognised as a tulku, but had not been officially confirmed because of the political situation, he was the obvious choice. At the age of ten Jamdrak left the bosom of his family to join Akong Tulku Rinpoche and begin his formal education at the bleak, remote monastery of Dolma Lhakang.

Jamdrak studied diligently, if reluctantly, under a succession of Lamas but at the age of fifteen his studies were rudely interrupted when the Chinese invaded Tibet. In 1959 the two young brothers, together with an older brother, several Rinpoches and a party of three hundred people, fled the monastery. They had been advised of the impending invasion by a very high Lama and warned to leave or they would be in danger of losing their lives. As the Chinese had occupied Lhasa, the party was forced to find an alternative route. A perilous journey across the Himalayas took them through frozen wastes, high mountain passes and raging rivers. Although they were on the point of death, the brothers were among thirteen people, out of the three hundred who had set out, who made it to the Indian border. The rest of their group had either died of starvation, been captured or killed.

Once in the heat and unfamiliar environment of India, many of the recently arrived Tibetan refugees fell sick. Jamdrak's elder brother died of TB and Jamdrak himself contracted both TB and smallpox. But following a major operation in which one of his lungs was removed, he recovered well and was able to resume his education. After passing his exams at the school for young tulkus he was chosen to join a group of gifted pupils being groomed for jobs as administrators of the new Tibetan settlements.

Following an audience with His Holiness the Dalai Lama, Jamdrak secured an important and well paid post as administrator for a large Tibetan settlement in southern India. However, this turned out to be short lived, as a meaningful encounter in New Delhi with His Holiness the 16th Karmapa irrevocably changed the young man's life. Seeing his potential, the Karmapa invited Jamdrak to join him at his monastery in Sikkim. Coming from a family of Kagyu Buddhists Jamdrak had great devotion to the Karmapa. He did not hesitate to give up his prestigious job and join His Holiness at Rumtek Monastery in Sikkim.

As a young lay person with a good education and reasonable English, Jamdrak found himself assisting the Karmapa in a secretarial capacity and also in the privileged position of receiving Buddhist teachings from the very highest Lamas. When Freda Bedi, the remarkable English woman who became ordained as Sister Palmo, arrived at Rumtek to take teachings from the Karmapa, Jamdrak acted as translator. He was allowed to take the initiations with Sister Palmo, given by Karmapa for the practices of Vajrayogini, Karma Pakshi and Gyalwa Gyamtso. Even though Jamdrak was not a monk he was nevertheless given a room alongside the four young regents of the Kagyu Lineage and was allowed to meditate and practise in a room of the temple that held all the precious relics of the Kagyupas. The Karmapa often referred to Jamdrak as his son and treated him in the same way as the high Rinpoches.

Despite his devotion to the Karmapa, Jamdrak did not fully appreciate this precious opportunity and, after coming into contact with some young American Peace Corps volunteers, he became curious about the West. Enlisting the help of his friend Chogyam Trungpa Rinpoche who, with Akong Tulku Rinpoche, had by this time set up Kagyu Samye Ling Tibetan Centre in Scotland, Jamdrak managed to cut through the Indian bureaucratic red tape and obtain a passport, visa and plane ticket to Britain in record time.

His arrival in Britain coincided with the sixties hippie movement. Young aristocrats, actors and pop stars were among those who flocked to Samye Ling and

Jamdrak lost no time in throwing himself into their exciting, hedonistic lifestyle. Meanwhile his brother Akong Tulku Rinpoche, who was busy running Samye Ling, patiently tolerated his younger brother's excesses, hoping he would grow out of them before long. Although his brother had given him everything, Jamdrak started to feel empty and dissatisfied inside. The turning point came after a fateful fishing trip to the Orkney's with a family friend.

As a Buddhist, Jamphel Drakpa wasn't happy with the idea of fishing, but had agreed to go so as not to disappoint his friend. Although he didn't know how to fish, the fish just found his hook and before long there was a large heap of them lying in the boat which his friend then killed by hitting them over the head. The friend was really pleased with their catch and, lining up all the dead fish, took pictures that he proudly showed to Akong Tulku Rinpoche on their return home.

For the first time in his life Jamdrak saw his brother Akong Tulku Rinpoche become visibly moved. His face was looked pained as he took the young rebel to one side, and his voice was full of sadness as he explained to Jamdrak how he had promised their parents that he would look after him. Akong Tulku Rinpoche said he had tried to be both mother and father to his brother and had always given him whatever he asked for. Although he had tried to bring Jamdrak up as a good Buddhist and a decent person, he felt that he had failed and was unhappy as he could not be at peace with their parents.

Jamphel Drakpa's heart was torn with anguish

and remorse. He realised how he had previously resented his brother, as if it were somehow his fault that they had been separated from their parents at a young age. In that instant he saw how kind Akong Tulku Rinpoche had always been, never refusing him anything and always giving him whatever he had. As he says in his own words, 'If he had beaten me it could not have been a worse pain than that which I felt at that time. His kindness could have changed the heart of a monster. From then on I was no longer interested in rebelling against him. I wanted to change and do something to make him happy and proud of me.'

Hearing that His Holiness Karmapa was going to America at the invitation of Chogyam Trungpa Rinpoche, Jamdrak requested Akong Tulku Rinpoche to allow him to go and be reunited with His Holiness and with the Dharma path. Akong Rinpoche complied and a chastened but determined Jamdrak went to join the Karmapa and his entourage on an extensive tour of the US and Canada.

Towards the end of the tour, His Holiness met a wealthy Chinese Buddhist benefactor who offered him a large tract of land in New York State for the purpose of establishing a Dharma centre. Much to his amazement, Jamdrak was appointed as Secretary and Treasurer of this project by the Karmapa, with another young Tibetan, Lama Tenzin Chonyi to be President. With the help of the Chinese benefactor Jamdrak and Lama Tenzin first rented a property in New York and invited several Tibetan Lamas over from India to begin giving teachings. Before long a new centre named Karma

Triyana Dharmachakra was set up in a peaceful, rural setting near Woodstock. With Khenpo Karthar Rinpoche, Bardor Tulku Rinpoche and Lama Ganga as resident teachers the Dharma began to flourish in New York State and in the reformed Jamdrak.

Whenever high Lamas such as Tai Situpa and Thrangu Rinpoche came to visit, Jamdrak would receive initiations and teachings. He also practised the Four Foundations under the guidance of Khenpo Karthar. His mind was no longer fascinated with the trappings of Western civilisation for he had seen that it did not bring any lasting happiness. Knowing that he could not help himself, his brother, or anyone else until he had established some clarity and stability of mind, Jamdrak determined that it was not enough to practise as a lay Buddhist. He needed to rid himself of worldly distractions by becoming a monk and going on retreat. When His Holiness Karmapa next visited the US, Jamdrak asked to be ordained.

In May 1980, on the auspicious day commemorating the Buddha's enlightenment, His Holiness the 16th Gyalwa Karmapa bestowed full Gelong ordination on Jamphel Drakpa and gave him the Dharma name of Gelong Yeshe Losal. The ordination ceremony took place at the Karma Triyana Dharmachakra Centre in the presence of many high Lamas, including Jamgon Kontrul, Ponlop Rinpoche, Bardor Tulku, Khenpo Khartar, and Lama Ganga. After spending his first week as a monk with His Holiness in Washington DC, Yeshe Losal said goodbye to Karmapa, for what turned out to be the last time. When he returned to the Centre his last act, before entering into strict retreat, was to offer all his possessions to His Holiness Karmapa.

Yeshe Losal had already completed the Four Foundation Practices three times. In order to further his practice in solitude he had chosen a comfortable retreat cottage with its own bathroom and kitchen. However, when the great master Kalu Rinpoche visited, he advised Yeshe Losal to throw himself into his practice one hundred percent. Kalu Rinpoche said there was no point in him locking himself away in his nice cosy retreat house only to dip his toes into the practice. He should immerse himself fully and be like Milarepa, practising with every bone in his body.

Following Kalu Rinpoche's advice, Yeshe Losal read the biography and the songs of Milarepa and was moved to tears by the great Yogi Saint's story. He heard how Milarepa had overcome all obstacles and suffered tremendous hardships in order to achieve complete enlightenment in a single lifetime. Yeshe Losal saw himself as a wild being who needed to purify and tame his mind. He knew it would take great effort so, as well as meditating, he did at least three hours of non-stop prostrations a day, wearing out three prostration boards in the process. With Khenpo Karthar Rinpoche as his mentor Yeshe Losal also received teachings from the highest Lamas of the Kagyu Lineage, including Jamgon Kontrul, who gave him the empowerment of White Tara, and Goshir Gyaltsapa from whom he received instructions in the Six Yogas of Naropa.

For the next five years Yeshe Losal practised

relentlessly, overcoming both outer and inner obstacles. The comfort and tranquillity of his retreat cottage had been shattered by the arrival of heavy machinery as building work began on the large temple that was to become the shrine room for the Centre. To make matters worse, the water and electricity connections were cut, so the bathroom and toilet were unusable. He was reduced to using a plastic camping toilet for a lavatory and standing outside in the rain when he needed a shower! To add to his trials his house became a wildlife sanctuary. A large beaver dug a home for himself underneath the floorboards, while racoons and skunks fought fierce battles that would leave stinking memories for days afterwards. His secluded retreat cabin had turned into a torture chamber!

Although noise from the building work shook his little retreat house to its foundations, he remembered the trials that Milarepa had endured and strengthened his resolve, determined to see the positive side of the situation. A little noise and inconvenience was a small price to pay, compared with the benefit of building a beautiful shrine room for a Dharma Centre where the Buddha's teachings would flourish and benefit many beings. Later, Kalu Rinpoche said of Lama Yeshe Losal that he was the inheritor of all his wisdom and was his main lineage holder.

After five years Lama Yeshe Losal was requested by Akong Tulku Rinpoche to return to Samye Ling where his other brother and sister had arrived from Tibet. Emerging from his retreat house, his body was almost skeletal, but his mind was crystal clear. He flew to Scotland to meet his family and was persuaded by Akong Tulku Rinpoche to resume his retreat at Samye Ling's purpose built Purelands Retreat Centre, rather than returning to the US.

Purelands had been established to accommodate practitioners entering the traditional Buddhist closed retreats lasting either four years or three years and three months. When the long retreat finished in 1988 Lama Yeshe continued his solitary meditation. But before the next one could take place, the buildings had to be expanded to accommodate over forty men and women who were waiting to take part. Consequently Lama Yeshe once again found himself meditating in the middle of a building site with people working all day for seven months in order to get the building finished in time. Lama Yeshe's porch became the storage place for building materials, including hundreds of bags of cement. As the dust entered his window and his one good lung he refused to let the constant noise and commotion disturb him and instead he would practise patience and attain the pure view, seeing the noise as the herald of a new retreat that would benefit many more people.

When the Retreat Master passed away, Akong Tulku Rinpoche asked his brother to take over the responsibility. Gradually, Lama Yeshe became spiritual advisor not only in the retreat but also at Samye Ling. As Akong Tulku Rinpoche's work for Rokpa Trust took him to Tibet and other countries for increasingly longer periods, Lama Yeshe became more involved in the daily running of Samye Ling. Many young Westerners were drawn to seek his advice and, having experienced their way of life, Lama Yeshe was ideally equipped to help them deal with their problems. In 1995 Akong Tulku Rinpoche requested Khentin Tai Situpa to formally appoint Lama Yeshe Losal as Abbot of Kagyu Samye Ling.

Having found peace of mind by becoming a monk and wholeheartedly practising meditation, Lama Yeshe felt others would also be able to benefit from similar experience. He knew that most Westerners would be unfamiliar with the idea of ordination, therefore he instituted a system whereby they could take vows as novice monks or nuns for one year. If, after their year was up, they wished to extend their vows they could then do so. In this way the number of western Sangha at Kagyu Samye Ling and its associated Centres has gradually grown to more than fifty monks and nuns, many of whom now have full ordination and a lifetime commitment. As well as practising meditation and engaging in Buddhist studies, Sangha are also involved in running the Centres. Unlike most Tibetan lamas, Lama Yeshe has no monastery to maintain in Tibet, he therefore considers Kagyu Samye Ling as his monastery and is fully committed to establishing the Sangha and continuing the lineage in the West.

In order to best help the people who turn to him for guidance, Lama Yeshe sees it as imperative to take time out from his busy schedule and enter into a period of intensive retreat each year. It was at Akong Tulku Rinpoche's suggestion that Lama Yeshe sought out the renowned but elderly meditation master, Tulku Urgyen

Rinpoche and requested the master to pass on the precious lineage of Bardo Retreat practice. Tulku Urgyen Rinpoche, sensing that Lama Yeshe would succeed where others had failed in this most difficult but effective practice, not only passed on the profound transmission but also allowed Lama Yeshe to use his own retreat hut.

Despite the primitive conditions of the tiny hut with its dirt floor, and lack of water, heat or light, with only a pipe through the roof to allow air to circulate, Lama Yeshe succeeded in accomplishing this most testing of practices with a clear and steady mind. Some years later, he repeated the Bardo Retreat in his own retreat cabin on Holy Island and is the only known living person in Europe to have twice completed the forty nine day Bardo Retreat in total darkness. This experience, together with his previous twelve years of solitary retreat, more than bore out the description of him that His Holiness the 16th Karmapa had given when he advised anyone who wished to learn meditation to look no further than Lama Yeshe Losal.

Lama Yeshe's wish for the Dharma to take root and blossom in the West was given fresh impetus when, in 1990, he was approached by an Irish lady who told him she owned an island in the Firth of Clyde. She wished to sell the island and had been guided by a vision of Mother Mary to approach the Buddhists of Samye Ling. And so, on a cold December day, Lama Yeshe sailed across from the Isle of Arran to the small but impressive Holy Island, gazing for the first time at its wild beauty and the imposing mountain of Mulloch Mor with its summit wreathed in mist.

Once ashore, Lama Yeshe felt an immediate affinity for the island's rugged terrain, so reminiscent of his lost homeland of Tibet. After exploring the island Lama Yeshe sat on the shore as night fell, looking out over the sea towards Lamlash on the Isle of Arran where street lamps lit up the bay like so many butterlamp offerings. It was then he remembered a vision he had seen years before while practising dream yoga in his retreat at Woodstock. He had experienced flying over a beautiful island that was surrounded by twinkling lights. Sitting on that shoreline ten years later, Lama Yeshe knew he had a strong connection to the island and should do everything in his power to acquire it.

Knowing its ancient history as a place of deep spiritual significance in pre-Christian and Celtic Christian times, Lama Yeshe felt inspired to reawaken the island's sacred past and develop it as place of refuge and retreat, not only for Buddhists, but for people of all faiths. In spite of a lack of funds, Lama Yeshe's vision for Holy Island was so strong that he was able to fire the imagination of others and after a massive fundraising effort the island was signed over to Rokpa Trust in April 1992.

Meanwhile, Lama Yeshe Losal's workload became increasingly full. Apart from his work at Samye Ling, Lama Yeshe travelled widely, teaching at Samye Dzongs and associated centres around the world. His non-denominational approach and easy manner also made him a popular speaker with other groups such as the Global Business Network who invited him to speak to the international business community. On one such occasion in Maastricht, Lama Yeshe Losal addressed a group of the top six hundred managers of Shell and was later praised by their Chairman as being the only person who had ever been able to keep these executives not only silent but also meditating for fifteen minutes!

Uniquely, Lama Yeshe Losal is also the only Tibetan Lama to have been honoured by Buddhists of the Theravadin tradition when, in November 1998, he was awarded the title of Sasana Kirti Sri, or Illustrious Renowned Teacher, at the Award Ceremony of the Sarvodaya Bikkhu Congress in Sri Lanka. In February 1998 he was invited to participate in an historic ordination ceremony for over one hundred nuns at the holy place of Bodgaya in India. As well as acting as one of the preceptors on this auspicious occasion, Lama Yeshe also took eleven of his own nuns to receive the full Bhikkuni or Gelongma vows, thereby enabling full ordination of nuns within the Tibetan Buddhist tradition.

Wherever he goes Lama Yeshe Losal tries to help people in whatever way is most useful for them. His non-judgmental nature and sunny temperament act like a magnet to people of all faiths and backgrounds, and never more so than when he enthuses about the Holy Island Project, which he sees as being of vital importance to the world as a whole. Lama Yeshe has overseen extensive conservation work on the island's environment and its existing buildings. Thirty thousand native trees have been planted, the buildings have been sensitively restored and organic gardens now grow much of the island's food. Holy Island is a haven for many precious species of flora and fauna and has also been officially designated as a Sacred Site by the ARC, (Alliance of Religions and Conservation).

Far away from the distractions of worldly life Holy Island was known as a spiritual place even before the 6th Century, when the Celtic Christian Saint Molaise spent a period of retreat there in a cave that has now become a place of pilgrimage. Lama Yeshe sees the island as the ideal place to establish a long term Buddhist Retreat Centre at the south end and an interfaith Centre for World Peace and Health at the north. With his ongoing work at Samye Ling, on Holy Island, at many international Samye Dzong Centres and with other groups too numerous to mention, Lama Yeshe Losal's selfless activity bears all the hallmarks of the true Boddhisattva. May his life be long and fruitful in order that he may continue to spread the Dharma and benefit all beings according to their needs.

I wrote this little poem for a young friend of mine who was mentally unwell, and put it here as an introduction to give you an idea of the subject of this book.

SKY

As you know the sky is very, very blue
And very, very transparent.
It has no centre or limitation.
So you see, your mind is like the sky.

But sometimes, you know, lots of clouds come into space
From nowhere,
With no warning.
But they also disappear just like they come.

Your thoughts and emotions are just like the clouds.
They come from nowhere.
But so long as you give them solidity,
They give you problems.

Sometimes, if there are lots of clouds, they create rain.
Just like this,
When you hold onto your emotions, give them solidity,
It gives you tears.

But if you can always remember your own Buddha Nature,
Which is limitless like space,
And let go of the cloud-like emotions,
You will be a very, very happy person.

Lama Yeshe Losal
Samye Ling
1st June, 2001

LIVING DHARMA

A practical guide to Buddhism
and its application in daily life

By Ven. Lama Yeshe Losal

LIVING DHARMA

Our hidden potential: Buddha Nature

The subject of this book is Buddhism and how to apply Buddhist principles to make your life happy and meaningful. Nowadays, some people are put off by just hearing the word 'religion', but Buddhism is not so much a religion as a philosophy or a way of life. Buddhism is timeless, very progressive and fits the ideas of this 21st century perfectly.

When searching for spiritual values, many people look for something very fresh and new, and think that Buddhism, which has been around for about 2,500 years, is too old. But that is not true! Buddhism is the freshest thing you'll ever come across, because our mind is constantly fresh, and the Buddha is talking about nothing other than our state of mind. He teaches that everything, whatever we experience, good or bad, happy or sad, all happens through states of mind. He's talking about our own mind, so how could we ever get anything fresher than that?

Buddhism teaches about equality: that differences in race, culture, tradition and belief do not really matter. The fundamental teaching in Buddhism is that everybody has the opportunity and possibility to become a Buddha. Every human being has this potential. The only difference between a Buddha and ordinary beings is that a Buddha has fulfilled it, whereas we are still searching. The Buddha did not keep his discovery to himself but, out of his love and compassion, he wished that all sentient beings might discover this inherent potential within themselves. This realisation, this recognition of our Buddha nature, is very important for all of us. To recognise it is to fully free ourselves, and to achieve this we need to concentrate on what will really free us instead of running after mirages that will never bring us complete and lasting happiness.

As far as I am concerned, Buddhism is the simplest and most practical religion in the world, because our body is ours, our speech is ours, our mind is ours - and our time is ours. All we need to do is learn how to use these properly in order to change our habits and improve ourselves.

When people come to realise that this modern materialistic way of life is meaningless, I think that they will gradually accept the Buddhist teachings, but I am definitely not trying to make a Buddhist out of anyone. Buddhism is very open and teaches respect for all other beliefs. People who have other beliefs might think that Buddhism has nothing to do with them, nothing to offer them, but Buddhism could actually mean everything to them. It could be the missing piece they have been looking for all their lives.

Buddhism tells us about our potential. This potential does not belong only to Buddhists, or only to Christians: it belongs to each and every human being with no distinction of faith, race or culture. We have to learn how to search for it, not 'out there' but right within ourselves. We don't need to go to any other person or believe in any other thing, the only important step is to believe in ourselves, in the potential we have within ourselves. When we talk about Buddhism, we are actually talking about the mind. If you do not want to hear about 'Buddhism', the 'Buddha' or 'enlightenment', we can leave out such words and talk only about the mind.

The most important thing is to learn to appreciate what we have. We really seem to forget how fortunate, how lucky we are. To be able to appreciate our lives, who and what we are, allows us to trust other people and also to have faith and devotion. It makes us wholesome human beings. If we don't appreciate what we have, then even if we have everything, we are still unhappy. We don't have peace of mind and it is impossible for us to trust anybody, not to mention having faith and devotion. Some people get so paranoid and lose self-confidence to the point that they cannot even trust themselves. This is why all the religions in the world first teach us to be humble, decent and honest. When we have those qualities, then everything becomes so simple, so easy!

I think that we should not get carried away with words like nirvana and realization. All this means nothing to people like us. What is nirvana? What is enlightenment? If we have found inner peace, then satisfaction comes, happiness comes, joy, generosity, the ability to trust, everything comes! It is all part of this inner peace. I always remind people that the religion they follow makes no difference. If their practice helps them become more humble, better human beings who are able to appreciate themselves and others, then I think they have achieved their goal!

Of course, we are all trying to find happiness. The problem is that we get so fooled by appearances. This 21st century is so 'visual'. Whatever has a physical form has such an impact on everybody. People want to see and enjoy beautiful things, yet they fail to see that these things are hollow inside. They want a good job, money and relationships, and they are able to change them like changing paper napkins, yet they are not happy. They are in fact looking for a direction that would give meaning to their lives but they fail to recognise that they are actually using poison in their search for happiness. It is impossible to obtain happiness through envy, jealousy, pride, anger and selfishness. If we plant poisonous seeds, the result will be inedible fruits.

This is why I think it is so important to learn to tame our mind. In a way, we have been fully tamed and trained by our own culture, by our traditions and family values, but these values are worldly values that are all about how to survive in this world. Nowadays, people are on the whole more educated and have more knowledge than ever in the past, but if we look at the world situation, we have to admit that all this education and knowledge is no good without inner wisdom as the guide.

We are living in a civilisation where people are brought up like sheep and instead of training their own minds, they either follow others or force others to go along with their ideas. We see it every day. There are many decent young people, even grown-up people, struggling to make their voices heard in order to improve the world situation but they lack the proper training and knowledge and so somehow use the wrong methods to try to get the right result. They stubbornly try to force their own solutions on others. Like these young people with good heart and motivation, who go through so many hardships just to end up in jail, whereas the multinational companies they are fighting usually seem to win, thanks to all the money and clever lawyers they have.

The Buddha who was wise and enlightened saw that it is impossible to change things in this way. He said we need more wisdom than that; it is no use trying to change everybody else, we need to change ourselves.

A crazy way of life

There are many human beings in the world who apparently have everything - a job, money, a partner, material comfort, but who are mentally very poor. They cannot share their wealth with others and are also unable to appreciate what they have. Someone who completely forgets what they already have and is always focusing on what they still need to get in order to be happy, is not a fortunate human being. Actually they are mentally very poor!

On the other hand, there are many people who seem poor, but who are very content and happy. Those people are mentally richer because they know how to appreciate their precious life with the meagre things they have. They have the ability to stop thinking about what they don't have and to appreciate what they do have. A good, stable, peaceful mind is the best wealth one can ever have, because that is something one can never lose. If we look back at how our ancestors lived, they led very simple lives and were quite stable, content and honest.

How the capitalist system is built is very, very clever, because people get the feeling that the harder they work and the more commitment they make, the greater rewards they will get, be it more money, a bigger car or a better house. But in my opinion that's precisely the moment they have sold themselves out, the moment they have lost their dignity. They can no longer be themselves, they are enslaved by what they want.

Many people say, 'I'm very successful, I'm Director of so and so', and they live in a big house and drive around in a flashy car. They seem to have a lot of money but in fact their car and house are mortgaged and the minute they lose their job, they also lose their house, their car and probably their relationship as well. That's how the world functions nowadays.

The unrestrained greed that drives so many people shows their lack of wisdom, their inability to appreciate what they have. Many people already have more than they could ever need, but although they have everything materially, they have no inner peace, no happiness. Some wealthy people do not even have time to eat a proper meal or to be with their children and husband or wife to share some kindness, warmth and happiness with them. They have big, beautiful houses but only find loneliness when they come home. The warmth they really need cannot come from electricity or central heating, it can only come from love and compassion. They are rich but their money is invested in stock exchanges and these days stock exchanges are having constant peaks of high fever - quotations fluctuate all the time. These rich people worry all day long and when they lose money, they are unable to eat, unable to sleep, unable to give anything away!

What human beings really need is loving kindness. Is this life meant to be lived only in the name of success and wealth? Do we have to torture ourselves twenty four hours a day to achieve it? If that is so, then there is something wrong in this world.

I have been to Third World countries and you have all seen it on TV, people living in poverty with only a few possessions, sometimes not even a roof over their heads. Their main worry is where the next meal is coming from. People here are very sympathetic and feel sorry for them. They give money and send food, clothes and medicines, which is very good but brings no lasting solution. As a Lama who has spent many years in Europe, I feel differently. I feel very sorry for those Europeans who have so much material wealth and the anxiety that comes from too much choice. When I see you running like ants every morning during the rush hour, not even looking around, most of you still half asleep, arriving at work without even having found the time to have breakfast, then spending the whole day chasing after things, I often wonder how you can survive such a way of life. What do you do this for?

Of course, everybody who is physically and mentally fit should work to earn their living. Laziness and depending on others to provide for one's needs is not acceptable; but doesn't your civilisation teach you that unrestrained greed is a great poison and the source of all your difficulties? Mentally you are losing yourselves. You may be physically well fed, but your Buddha nature within is starving to death because you don't take the time and don't have the wisdom to achieve peace in your mind.

Therefore I feel that maybe many of you need more help than those poor people you watch on television and feel sorry for. Because where is your happiness? In New York City, in London, and in all big Western cities, neighbours don't even know each other. People are so paranoid and emotional! They distrust other human beings and do not even trust themselves!

I'm not talking about all these things negatively, but that is how life seems to function here, isn't it? To lead a decent life, to feel happy and positive, it seems to me that we really should be gentler and kinder towards ourselves, which would result in our being kinder towards others. We should know when to get up, we should have plenty of time to have breakfast, plenty of time to talk to our family, and then go to our workplace gently and happily!

If Westerners were wise, they would know by now that money doesn't bring lasting happiness. All the freedom they think they have has not brought them any benefit, or at least it seems to me to give them more problems than benefits.

I think that the Western world, with its high standards, high income, good education and health care, is in the best position to say, 'Stop! Enough is enough!' We have enough wealth to share around so that every human being in the West might lead a simple but decent, pure lifestyle, with enough food to eat, a roof over their head, decent clothes to wear. That's all that counts. There's no need to kill yourself to get more than that. Because what will you do if you die suddenly? You won't be able to take along any of these wonderful things you have worked so hard for all your life. You can take nothing with you, not even your beloved body, so what's the use of all this rat race mentality?

It is time for people to pursue spiritual values instead of materialistic values because the way things are going now is like a big motorway going downhill, upon which cars without drivers roll at full speed. You now have the choice between two alternatives. You can let things roll on downwards until a huge disaster - some may call it a blessing - leaves you no choice, or you can apply wisdom and put a brake on it. Otherwise this inner insecurity is going to grow every second!

When I first came to Europe thirty years ago, it was very important to get a good education and a job that would last for life. Today, where is your secure job for life? Modern technology changes so quickly that the human mind cannot keep pace with it. Thirty years ago, it would take many months for an architect to draw plans for a building and he would be confident of keeping his job and feeling secure. Now, that job can be done within a few hours by a computer. Our minds cannot keep up with the new technologies.

In the past, human beings were asked to compete with other human beings. It could be stressful because some were not good at competing or were not capable enough, but now we are asked to compete not with human beings but with machines! How can we ever hope to have a peaceful, content mind when our productivity by hand is so small and machines can do everything? How can we compete with machines and think that we can maintain our former life style? When I look at it, I see that more and more people are going to be mentally unfit, which will result in more and more people being physically very sick. Mankind cannot keep up with machines. We are not machines; we are human beings. This way of life doesn't make sense. It doesn't make us any happier.

As a small child, you are told by your parents how to behave, and you receive a good education in school where you are taught what to pursue in life. Yet you never really get the foundation you actually need. You can pursue things for your whole life, go through hardships and sufferings to obtain them, get aged and wrinkled and still not be happy.

This whole civilisation is like a huge sandcastle. As long as you have a job, relatives, belongings, you feel all right. The moment you lose them, you start moaning and suffering. The Buddha said that this life is based on suffering because we constantly pursue and chase what we think we must have to be happy. For instance - maybe this is a monk's point of view and not everybody will agree - since I do not want to have a relationship, when I am alone, I don't feel lonely. Whereas if your whole life is geared towards your relationships with others, when you're alone, you feel very lonely and unhappy.

Desire and attachment are the source of all our sufferings. If there was no attachment, losing things wouldn't be so painful, but how can we hope to have the whole world and keep it when we cannot even keep our dear body alive? Life is too short to go on chasing after things and suffering.

We should know that all aspects of our life are a mental manifestation and that everything is a question of mental attitude. Happiness and sufferings all come from the mind. If we know this, why should we let our wisdom be trampled by greed and desire?

We should learn to meditate, to increase our discernment and our wisdom as to what is necessary and what is unnecessary. We should analyse our situation, start appreciating what we are and stop chasing the things everybody else is chasing after. If we are able to have a very good relationship with our family and friends, if we have a peaceful mind, that is wealth! Material wealth cannot even be called wealth, because we can have everything and lose it all from one moment to the next. Therefore we should really concentrate on discovering our wonderful inner potential - the Buddha nature I talked about in the beginning - and on becoming truly and completely free.

Freedom and responsibilities

Knowing that we have this great potential, we naturally aspire to freedom. But freedom comes with responsibilities. Many people in the West are very proud to say: 'We live in a free world, we are free!' whereas in fact - from my point of view - they are not. It is true that they are given permission to think, speak and act as they wish, but when such freedom is not supported by wisdom, human beings can behave worse than animals. Although human beings are unique and intelligent, when they lack wisdom, they often misuse their so-called freedom for the wrong purpose. They abuse their mind, their speech and their capacity to act. For me, giving such so-called freedom to people who don't have the right knowledge and the right training is like giving sharp knives to children. What can a child do with a sharp knife? He will either hurt himself or hurt others. According to my view, such 'freedom' doesn't really mean too much. You are legally empowered to be free, but within yourself, you are not free at all!

Most people want to be free but don't want to take responsibilities. But freedom is inseparable from responsibility! If I have the freedom to think, it is my responsibility to think positively. If I have the freedom to speak, it is my responsibility to speak properly and meaningfully. If I have the freedom to act, it is my responsibility to act correctly. Nobody else can take that decision for me. If every human being could feel responsible in that way, the world would be a better place. But most of us do not take any responsibility for what we say, think and do. We always find excuses for ourselves and put the blame on others or on circumstances. It is of course easier to blame others but, according to the Buddha's teachings, this will not work, we are at least as responsible as the person we blame.

In Buddhism, we talk about 'karma'. Some people do not want to hear that word and say they do not believe in karma. But instead of calling it 'karma', we can just call it 'cause and effect' and the meaning becomes very simple. If I punch somebody, he will punch me back. If I say bad things about other people, they will say bad things about me. Everything we think, everything we say, everything we do, has consequences. It means we know that whatever we do will produce effects that we will experience. It is like cultivating a field. If we plant pure seeds, we will have a pure crop, but if we sow weeds, we will produce weeds, not a pure crop. We can only clean a field by going into it and picking up the weeds one by one. We can only 'weed out' our mind by meditating and facing our negative emotions, no matter how painful the process may be.

When I look at what is happening these days throughout the world, I wonder how people can ever trust and believe someone else when they don't even trust themselves, when they don't even know what's going on in their own minds? They don't know themselves well enough. Many people who are mentally not doing very well only talk about their problems and pains, but the minute they get proper help and feel better, they are afraid. Even when they could experience some happiness, they reject it because they think they do not deserve it. Their ego pushes them in the wrong direction. If one really thinks one doesn't deserve happiness, why then worry so much about what happens, why complain and why not allow oneself some happiness? Some people are completely wrapped up in pain and suffering, but actually they don't want to let go of that pain. They identify with the suffering. Most people are afraid of introspection because they feel they have so much unwanted information in their heads, so much unhappiness, that they don't want to deal with it.

In this way, people project everything onto others and never accept anything as their own responsibility. They always find ways and means to put the blame on everybody else. But practising Buddhism means taking responsibility for ourselves, which means we cannot blame someone else. And if we follow the Buddhist path for a while, we may come to see that there isn't even any 'me' in the first place to experience such a pain. We solidify the 'I', and this 'I' then comes with pleasure and pain. How can we blame others if there is no 'me'? It is 'me', this big ego, who's making judgements. Other people are like mirrors. If we have no mirror, how can we see our reflection? We cannot put the blame on others or on circumstances and take no responsibility for ourselves.

This is very easy to understand and it helps us to see the necessity of practice and meditation, of learning to think, speak and act positively and meaningfully, of developing our potential properly. Otherwise we become a crazy and harmful race.

Looking back in history, Buddha, Christ and all the

great teachers recognised their potential and used it. They took full responsibility in perfecting their potential and now, 2500 years later, we are still benefiting from their taking this responsibility. Other human beings had exactly the same potential but used it the wrong way. It has recently caused two World Wars, cost millions of lives and brought misery to many more. We can clearly see the difference. The former brought benefit, happiness and everlasting knowledge to their fellow human beings. The latter, misguided, ignorant and lacking wisdom, used their potential to destroy life and we don't even want to remember their names.

In order to take full responsibility for our actions, our speech and our thoughts, it is essential to see that it's time for all of us to tame and train our body, speech and mind.

Taming the body

To train the body is relatively easy because physical actions are easy to see and to recognise. Our body is the first thing that involves us in the world, because it has a form, it has some sort of solidity. We do many things with our bodies and we all have many weird habits. Someone may go through different levels of emotional turmoil, but the first sign of the neurosis will be, for instance, slamming doors, or dropping plates in the kitchen. Such actions are very easy to notice. We should try not to react so strongly and so quickly at the first emotional impulse. Our mind is the boss, the body follows it's instructions, therefore we should be mindful, check our actions and try to overcome such habits.

Walking heavily and being noisy can disturb others. Hurting them is not what we really want. Learning to move slowly and gently can take some time, but it is possible and we should try to achieve this out of respect for others. Ordinary people will argue that this is taking their freedom away from them because they should be allowed to 'express their feelings' freely. This is what I call a shallow world. Expressing every feeling of yours in a wrong way doesn't do anybody any good. You should be aware that the moment you express something, it affects others. Remember causes and effects!

To tame ourselves is the only way we can change

and improve the world. This means we should always remember never to hurt any being through our physical form, never to do any wrong physical action. Taming the activities of the body is very easy. Sometimes people think it's difficult, but it's not. Human beings train animals by teaching them, beating them, giving or denying them food or even giving them electric shocks! Lions are not meant to jump like they do in the circus. If we are able to tame animals, then how come we can't train our own body? It is more crucial to train ourselves than to train animals, because human beings are the cause of the world's problems, not animals.

Taming the speech

We need to tame the simple physical form, but the most lethal weapon I've seen used by people is speech! This is actually worse than machine guns. People use their speech to twist everything around. It's used almost every day by everybody to separate friends, to send wrong information, to hurt other people. Trying to build up a good friendship can take so many years and just a few words can ruin it in seconds. Words can hurt so much. They can sometimes be very harmful. Being human beings means we have enough intelligence to know that giving unnecessary pain and suffering to others is not the right way. Just as we don't like to be abused, other people don't like to be abused either.

I often look at the world and wonder why things are getting so bad. According to Buddha's teachings, we have lost respect for honest, true people. We ignore those who are honest and truthful, whereas liars, cheats and people who have a big mouth, are in high positions everywhere. So the world is changed in the wrong way. We are therefore also partly responsible for what is going on, because we don't have the wisdom to appreciate and value people who are wise, learned, honest and truthful. In traditional cultures, a truthful person's speech has value. A truthful person doesn't need to say very much, but people will respect his or her words. They know they'd better listen to so and so because he or she really speaks the truth. On the other hand, untruthful persons can talk all day and night but people won't value their words, because they know they're lying all the time and their speech has lost its meaning and its value.

In this modern world, we just turn everything upside down through our lack of wisdom. We know that the politicians make a lot of promises, and that they will not be able to deliver, but still we vote for them because we have a 'good feeling' for them, or because they talk so well.

For me, training our speech means learning to speak the truth, always being careful not to use speech to cause chaos or to bring more suffering into the world. If we can always remember this, then the gift of speech is really meaningful.

Taming the Mind

Taming the mind is more difficult than training the body or speech. Mind has such a big potential! It's the mind that gives you pleasure, happiness and joy, as well as pain, sorrow and unhappiness, - everything! If you really look into where your emotions start, where they come from, you will see they all have to do with your state of mind. For instance, when you feel mentally very stable, physically very well, if people abuse you or give you a hard time, at that specific moment, you will feel it's no problem, you can accept it, it doesn't hurt you, it's no big deal. But if you are physically and mentally not so well, then you become so negative that people don't even need to say anything wrong, you will get upset even if they say the right things to you. This shows that what matters is not what we say or do, but our state of mind.

To tame one's mind is the most difficult thing, but also the most essential. We can never be truly happy or peaceful without taming the mind. Therefore we should not feel afraid or overwhelmed by the task, but simply resolve to begin and stick with it. This is why we meditate.

The rest of this book is devoted to explaining how and why we should tame our minds in order to truly benefit ourselves and others. In the following chapters we will go through this process stage by stage.

Developing our inner potential

If people really want to benefit from the Buddhist teachings, meditation is the right way to achieve that goal. To discover our potential to become Buddhas, all we really need is to allow ourselves some time and some space to sit down and relax, physically and mentally. We should at least find the time to sit for fifteen minutes in a quiet room every morning, think about what we are going to do during the day and always remember to be very careful with our body, speech and mind.

Sometimes people say they have a job, a family and so many things to do that they can never find time to practise, but that's not really wise. Maybe you know deep down in your mind that learning to practise is the only thing that can help you to stabilise your mind and give you a direction, some sort of purpose in your life. If everybody else is crazy, what's the good of you getting crazy as well in this mad world? You see everybody running, therefore you also start running, without thinking properly, without much of a goal, except getting some money and a job. That's a crazy world! We human beings are supposed to have more abilities than animals. We can decide what we want to do, we can plan our lives, but it needs time and commitment.

There's a real benefit in trying to find even fifteen minutes every day to sit and meditate. It will transform you into a very positive human being. If you take some time to meditate in the morning and see how you can tame your mind and transform your habits, in the end you will see a real change. The minute the old habit starts, your mind will send you a message, 'Oh, you're not supposed to do this!' so that you are able to stop it. For instance, if you decide to use your speech in a more meaningful way to bring joy and happiness, whenever gossip or harmful words start to come, you will become aware of it and be able to stop, thus avoiding harm to others and causing more chaos.

It's so fortunate to be able to really change oneself. That's actually what we should do before trying to change the whole world. As long as we're unable to change ourselves, talking about changing others will have no result. We won't influence anybody. But if we are able to change ourselves, we won't need to preach anything, everybody will notice the change. Everybody will see that we are now able to cope with our life better than other people, that we have control over our actions and speech. That's the time when people will naturally get influenced and try to change their own ways.

It is therefore essential that we find the motivation and develop the willingness to learn to tame our mental activities. If we're really convinced that it's important to find this inner peace that nobody can take away from us, we will find the time. Time can always be found because when we like something, time is never a problem, there's never any shortage of time when we wish to gossip or entertain ourselves. Wouldn't it be much better for us to be at peace within ourselves, with no need to rely on another person or organisation, rather than constantly having to rely on somebody, someone, some place?

To learn meditation is not easy because nowadays people are so unhappy and angry. The minute we sit down and try to meditate, our neuroses and emotions take over. This is why, instead of trying to find inner peace, we usually let ourselves destroy other people's happiness because it is much easier. Destroying everybody else, blaming everybody else, is much easier than taking the blame on ourselves. However, we know that when we are calm, peaceful and stable, we are a kinder, gentler person. Any of us could be that wonderful person if we only had the wisdom to develop inner peace.

What Lamas like me are trying to do is to help you create that inner peace, help you to understand why it is beneficial and provide you with the proper information on how to proceed.

Meditation is the key to fulfilment

Wherever I go, I try to help beginners to learn the right way to start meditating, and to show those who think they are really advanced and know all about meditation that there is still a lot of room for improvement. According to the practice lineage, if one is able to practise Buddhism wholeheartedly, properly, meditation is one's food, meditation is one's partner, meditation is one's wealth, meditation fulfils every aspect of one's needs and wants!

Milarepa was a very famous Tibetan Yogi who lived in the 11th century - I hope many of you have read his life story and songs. When he was meditating in the mountains, his body turned green because he had nothing to eat except nettles. The king of Nepal once invited Milarepa, offering him great wealth, but he refused. Milarepa told the king that he was actually richer than him because he didn't need anything.

We are mentally very rich when we desire nothing. According to my experience, it is very good to really take to heart the notion that meditation can completely fulfil our every need, however difficult this idea may be to adopt in the beginning. Compared to a person who is very successful, who has a job, a wife, money, children, then I, a monk, have none of these, but if you compare our respective states of mind, I am much wealthier than this person because I have nothing to lose. As I have nothing to lose, I have no fear. When you have things, you are afraid of losing them. When you desire a wonderful thing, you are jealous of those who have it and once you have it, you must protect it. I have none of these, so I'm a most satisfied human being. What do I need? Just some simple food to sustain me and a roof above my head. I'm happy wherever I am. I can go to any part of the world, it makes no difference to me. I'm at peace with myself all the time. This is all due to this wish-fulfilling mind: it fulfils everything. I've found all the things I need. I don't have to chase what I want out there. I have found it right here, in my own mind. That's why I'm free.

For me, meditation is the best teaching any teacher can give. People in Buddhist centres may tell me, 'Don't teach meditation, because people don't like it and will run away!' But if we only talk, talk, talk, and none of us meditates, then what change is ever going to take place?

In my view - as I have understood from my own guru - simplicity, dedication, faith, and never giving up meditation practise even for one day, that is what really matters. Meditation is like food: one has to take it every day. So many people are practising as if they were having peaks of fever! When they feel very good, they can meditate for one, two or three hours but when they feel low, they totally give up practising, just when they need it most. We need to develop steadiness through regular daily practice.

Simplicity

For absolute beginners, the first meditation session is actually the first time they start to know themselves better. Initially, one should not have too great expectations. Some people may hope to learn how to leave all their pain and suffering, all their worldly concerns behind. Or they may wish to have beautiful or extraordinary experiences. However, we don't meditate in order to have experiences. In fact we really don't need experiences, as they can be a distraction.

Some may also be very curious and excited at the prospect of learning about 'Mahamudra' because they have heard it is the best, the highest meditation practice. However, I am quite sure many of them will be disappointed to discover that, in a way, the essence of Mahamudra is just to learn to accept everything the way it is. This sounds very simple but in fact it is the most profound practice of all. The Mahamudra approach makes our practice so simple that there isn't actually anything we need to worry about. Everything can be included into the practice so that everything we do participates in our spiritual path. This teaching is therefore about how we can become wise in using every moment.

To begin with, people in the West have a very complicated lifestyle. They have very busy jobs and very busy minds. Therefore people often think that only very complicated teachings will benefit them. I would rather say that their mind is already complicated enough and that the Dharma doesn't have to be complicated. It should be simple and easy to understand, in order to bring real benefits!

Sometimes, when simple instructions do not work, Lamas skilfully give you complicated visualizations to channel your strong mind energy. They allow you to be busy but not in your usual confused way. Most of the time, people just daydream; they don't realize how much daydreaming they do. But if you know how to daydream the right way, using visualization practices, it's much more meaningful. That allows you to gain stability, clarity and wisdom. This is 'guided' busy-ness, transforming your worldly busy-ness into spiritual busy-ness. Then, after such hard work, you may come to appreciate resting for a few minutes in simplicity. These are skilful methods devised to help you reach your inner self.

Maybe some of you might feel regret when, after twenty years of practice, you gain some realisation and understand that you didn't need to search after so many different things. You read hundreds of books, attended so many teachings and classes, and filled up your cupboards with everything you considered a teaching from all the different schools. You may understand that you wasted much time with all these complications and should instead have accepted the simplicity of the way things are.

Teachings and meditation are basically supposed to change our mind. They are supposed to help us when we die. I don't think we will be able to say to the Lord of Death, 'Wait a minute. I first have to look for instructions in my books!' The whole purpose of practising is for the Dharma to really become a part of our life, then we really benefit from it. Otherwise, we will become disillusioned and lament that we went to every school, met all the Holinesses and Eminences and didn't get any better or happier. It is as if we went to see many doctors but never took the medicines they gave us! We put them in our cupboards. How can anybody ever get better like that?

One of the great texts of the Mahamudra tradition says that we should see ourselves as a patient, meditation as the medicine and the Lama as the doctor. I don't mean by this that you are sick, but that you do need to take your daily dose of medicine, your meditation, otherwise you will only be looking outwards at the outside world without ever being able to actually deal with your own inner on-going chaos.

Working on ourselves

Books on Buddhism always mention 'non-grasping', 'non-attachment', 'letting go', being 'non-judgmental'. Most people think that 'non-attachment' concerns objects, possessions, relationships. They find such notions wonderful and think they can afford not to be attached to objects or persons, that they will be able to chuck out something or someone they don't want any more, to let go of something they feel is not useful for them. However, letting go actually means letting go of our emotions, letting go of our thoughts, feelings and self-identity. We are not dealing with objects in meditation, we are dealing with thoughts and emotions, we are dealing with our mind, we are working on ourselves.

For a meditation master, teaching is a difficult and tricky business because one has to talk about the mind. We all have the same mind. Therefore when one speaks about mind, everybody thinks that the Lama is talking to or about them, revealing their hidden defects, maybe even insulting them! People could take it personally and get frightened.

Basically, the idea of modern civilization being based on sensitivity and kindness is very good. However, if sensitivity is based on selfishness, it becomes harmful. Sensitivity means we should be sensitive to other people's feelings, and not be so over-sensitive ourselves that we cannot even hear what is right. We should develop 'wise sensitivity', which means that our actions should not cause any harm to other people. The wrong way is to be so sensitive that we pick up whatever others say thinking it applies to us - and get hurt. But the mind has the same quality for everybody, so Lamas are not saying anything to hurt you. However, in European languages, there is the saying, 'Truth hurts.' Therefore, if you feel hurt, it may mean that I said something useful, over which you need to reflect.

It is always instructive to see why we were able to make a connection with a teaching, be it through pain or through joy. If one comes to a teaching with the wish to hear what one wants, and if the teacher always tries to please his audience by saying what his students want to hear, what benefit will it bring to them? None! No one will change in the slightest way because the teacher is propping up his students' egos and they feel that everything is how it should be: they are getting what they want. I don't think that's the right way to teach Buddhism. Refusing to hear what you don't want to hear can be a problem for you.

As far as I am concerned, I am a meditator, I don't need to have students, I don't need any wealth. I am spiritually very wealthy without all this. There is nothing I lack. From my point of view, the only way to teach is to talk the truth and if people tell me, 'Lama Yeshe, maybe your teachings are wrong because you are losing students', then this will be the signal that it is time for me to go into retreat to meditate. Why should I waste my time going around talking when it is not useful to mankind? I feel I have a responsibility. For instance, after thirty years, I am still trying to learn your culture, your traditions, your beliefs so that whenever my help is required, I not only rely on my experience of Buddhism and meditation but also on a certain understanding of your way of life.

It is very difficult for Tibetan people to come here and start a European Sangha. Why would Tibetan Lamas actually come here to start a Sangha? In Asia there is a monastic tradition already so it is easy. When I was young I was living just like you, doing the same things, but when I got a little older, I gained some sort of wisdom and found a great teacher. I also have a good brother, and both guided me away from wrongdoings. I see now that my experience of your culture was very meaningful and useful. I can now fill the gap and reach Western people, because I can understand what you're going through. I can reach out to you. If I had been a monk all my life, if I hadn't had any connection with the Western lifestyle, if I hadn't had any opportunity to understand your culture and traditions, I wouldn't be able to really help you very much. I would be thinking my way and you would be thinking your way, and it would be very difficult to make any connection. But having gone through what I went through before and being what I am now, I feel I can be like a bridge. I can genuinely help.

When I became a monk, I never thought of becoming a teacher. It wasn't my ambition but sometimes karma has very strange ways: it seems that there are things we have to do. If I were given the opportunity, it would be no problem for me to be completely alone. But when I became a monk, it was certainly my commitment to help others as well as myself. As a teacher, I can either help people by teaching or help myself by meditating. I will definitely not play any so-called 'game'. Every human being plays a game all his or her life, but teacher and students should not play such a game. Therefore, I'm always thinking that wherever I go, even in Samye Ling, if people like me, fine. But if they don't like me, that is also fine. It makes no difference to me. I have no hidden desire to have a big place, many students or lots of money. That was never my dream.

If you come to a course and your mind resists what you hear, if you don't want to accept what the Lama teaches, I would say that, in a way, this mental rejection is quite natural because that is how your mind has somehow managed to survive in this world. It has always reacted in terms of its own interests, of protecting itself against any outer threat. But meditation does not enter that pattern. I can only give you advice. When I'm teaching, I'm not telling anybody what to do. To think that I am ordering anybody around is totally wrong. A Lama is asked to share knowledge and to give advice. If you think that what I say is suitable, that it is something you might like to try, then you can take it home with you. If you find it is not suitable, not right for you, then you can just leave it. Therefore, when I talk about the mind, I'm not talking to a specific group or a specific individual, I just talk about the mind, which is the same for everybody. The essence of mind is the Buddha nature, which is identical for everyone.

Of course, individual people have individual habits. All habits are different, which is why each individual has their own personality, ideas and feelings. But the essence of mind is one and the same for all. That is why the Buddha said that there is no fundamental difference between a Buddha and ordinary beings - they all have the same potential.

What is this mind? Mind is very strange. It gives us all the happiness, joy, pleasure, excitement, sadness and sufferings that we experience. One cannot say it has eyes or legs, yet it seems to see everything and to be all over the place. If one sends it away, it won't go; if one summons it to stay, it won't stay. We can try to mix it with things, but it doesn't seem to blend in with anything. There is nothing we can do with it. We cannot send it off, we cannot mix it with anything and it is all over the place.

Taming the mind is very difficult, most difficult! That's why so many people complain they are unable to meditate. If you're asked to move an object, you happily move it from here to there, confident that you have achieved something. But this mind can't be seen, so how can you move it? That's why many people think that those who meditate do nothing, that they are useless and would be better off doing something more meaningful, more useful. They think this because they don't know that sitting in meditation for a long period of time is more painful than 'doing' things as they do. They don't know that meditation can help us identify and fight our true enemy, which is much more difficult. Our real enemy is our wrong view, our own ego. In Tibetan we it call 'marigpa': ignorance.

'Marigpa' means not seeing what we call 'thamal shepa', the ordinary mind. From a Buddhist point of view, being ignorant is being unable to see things clearly. Once we are able to see things clearly, we achieve our goal. We could say that we now have 'worldly eyes' and should somehow open up our 'spiritual eyes', but we can only do this through purification, through meditation, through practice.

When one tries to find out what the mind is, one finds nothing. Some Asians identify the mind with the heart, but the heart is not the mind. Westerners identify it with the brain, but the brain isn't the mind either. To say that it doesn't exist because we cannot pinpoint anything as being the mind, is also no solution, because we experience it every moment.

As far as finding our true nature is concerned, we will only be able to see it when our 'ordinary mind' is able to see itself. Until then we'll remain more or less in darkness. But when one is really meditating, one can wholeheartedly connect with what Buddha said about our Buddha nature, or about our mind being all-pervading and having every capacity, every potential if it is used in the right way.

Mind is like space, because it has no limitation. When there are no clouds, when it is completely clear, space is like our 'ordinary' state of mind. Then, all of a sudden, clouds come from nowhere. Our emotional problems and mental chaos are like the clouds. When they take over, we can't see space any more, we only see the clouds! However space never goes anywhere, it's always there. It's just our mind getting into darkness so that, for us, the clouds become our only reality. It means that we give more solidity to our emotional upheavals, to all the things going on in our mind, so that they become more 'real' for us than the true essence of our mind. And as we have a physical form, when we get very emotional, the end result may be... tears rolling down our cheeks, just like rain falling from the clouds!

In a way, this is a very good example. I'm not saying it is the way it is, but there is a similarity. In the same way as clouds come from nowhere and disappear nowhere, our emotions and all the chaos we go through also somehow appear from nowhere and disappear into nowhere. Understanding this process, we should give it less value. Even if we've been under the clouds for seven days, we should always remember that space is there! Our true nature is there all the time; it's never gone! This will give us the confidence that clouds are not going to take us over forever. They're just temporary obstacles. Nobody is free from going through emotions and different problems sometimes, and practitioners need to learn how to deal with them. There is no need to think this is the end of our life: these are just temporary obstacles. It will help us to remember that nothing can happen to our true Buddha nature. It is pure, it is transparent, it is unpolluted and cannot be affected by anything. But it is temporarily hidden by our habitual tendencies, which we will be able to remove by purification, practice and meditation.

In Buddhism, we compare the mind to space, because even the Buddha could not see it. We think we see space, but we actually cannot even imagine its depth. Space has no limits: it cannot be measured. Mind is similar to space: it has the same qualities. The sky is there, unfathomable, yet we accept it as it is. Similarly, the only way we can somehow get along with this mind seems to be just a simple acceptance of the way it is. We can never find a solution to our investigation by just listening to teachings or reading books. The only way we can get closer to the nature of mind is through direct experience, and that is through meditation.

Spiritual paths and worldly ways

Right now in the world, there are many schools and many individuals teaching meditation but their aims seem to be very limited. Their main purpose seem to be to find inner peace, or sometimes some kind of excitement or good experiences through physical manipulations of the subtle energies. Some schools even teach you how to use your mind to excite your own desire, because they see that it's what people want and they are willing to give such techniques to increase desire! Actually this type of meditation doesn't help you at all, on the contrary, it makes your life more miserable.

As to the meditation schools that simply show you how to find peace, what is remarkable about just finding some peace or having some pleasurable experiences? If your aim is limited to finding peace and tranquility, you may, after fifteen years of meditation, find a certain peace of mind while sitting on your cushion, but you haven't dealt with your inner poisons, with the root of your emotional upheavals. As long as you're sitting, you may think you are very peaceful, very relaxed, but as soon as you go out and a challenge comes your way, you flare up in anger and you're worse than ever. That means you have just continued to prop up your ego and self-interest with no wider purpose.

We cannot afford to sit and do nothing for our whole life. We may find some peace but nothing else, no real fulfilment, because we have never planted any proper 'seeds'.

On the other hand, if we root out negative emotions and develop loving kindness, forgiveness and compassion, we benefit not only ourselves, but also our relatives, friends and the whole human race, all sentient beings.

Buddhism has many methods to calm the mind and Tibetan Buddhism in particular has a wealth of techniques that are unique and profound. The speciality of Vajrayana is that we are not trying to by-pass our emotional turmoil, have some sort of little peaceful time and that's all. We want to get rid of the root of our sufferings. We want to deal with the poisons. If we are able to root them out, then we have gained a real peace of mind and nobody can create chaos in our mind any more. People can call us any name, they can give us any hard time they want, but as we have dealt with the source of anger, they cannot destroy or take away the inner peace we have gained through practice.

In ordinary life, everything we do is serving our own interests, whereas in Vajrayana, we practise with selflessness. The path of Dharma does not have to be the same as the worldly path. Selfish ideas have no place here any more. It is therefore very important to know how to plant the right seeds in order to reap the right fruits, which is why we start any practice by planting the seed of Bodhicitta.

Bodhicitta and loving kindness

Before any practice, we say that, like the Buddhas of the past, present and future, we dedicate ourselves to the liberation of all sentient beings. In the same way that we don't want to suffer, we don't want these beings who have once been our close relatives and friends to suffer either. This means that we are not going to be happy by just finding a certain personal peace of mind. It is absolutely essential to remember that we spend all this time and energy in our practice to bring about positive results, the benefit and the change that everybody needs. We take the commitment to bring liberation to all beings, and we can only plant this seed when we have a Mahayana motivation.

Sometimes, when people are not well, they are not only angry at the whole world but they are also angry with themselves. This attitude doesn't make the world better. They create an environment that is not healthy for a 'wise' level of mind. Instead of planting poisoned seeds of anger and hatred, those who tread the Bodhisattva's path should plant the nourishing seeds of loving kindness. The Buddha said that his foremost, his most important teaching was unconditional love and compassion. A Bodhisattva's loving kindness is unconditional, which means that he or she is willing to give love without expecting anything in return from others. They do not help someone because they want something out of it, but out of overwhelming kindness and the unconditional wish to help those who really need help, free from any expectation. As there is nothing they want for what they give, there are no 'strings' attached to the gift. That is pure help. Whether or not you help out of pure generosity depends on your motivation. Expecting something for your help is like giving a spoonful of honey but mixing it with poison.

Nowadays, many people think that meditation is useless because they feel they are 'doing nothing' when they could be helping others 'out there'. Many decent people believe this. They genuinely want to help others but, more often than not, they have no inner stability, no wisdom. They have no clue how first to help themselves. Most of the time, they are actually bringing more chaos into the world. When someone who cannot swim jumps in the water to rescue those who are drowning, nobody is rescued; they all die! The whole purpose of meditation and practice is to develop greater strength, to become stable, healthy, confident and wise. If we have inner peace and wisdom, we will be well equipped to really help others unconditionally.

I don't consider that, for an intelligent human being in this part of the world, being able to look after oneself is a big deal any more. Anybody can do that. An intelligent human being, I mean someone with wisdom, is someone who is able to nourish their mind. If we are mentally happy, then physically we will be much healthier. But if we are not mentally happy, we will never be physically healthy. In Europe you have so many alternative therapies, so many people involved in helping others gain some sort of well-being. There may be some short term benefit, but in the long run one needs to work on one's mind. Our state of mind is so unstable that our thoughts and emotions are like feathers blown in all directions by samsara's strong wind. What choice do we have? Some people think they want to really make a commitment to this religion or that organization, but a few days or months later, they meet other people, make another choice and follow another path. We are offered such a wide range of choice, but it doesn't seem to make our lives better. It's like a supermarket. We have so much choice with food, but how much of it all can we eat? We end up throwing so much away! Too much choice doesn't make us happy, in fact it can make us more miserable and confused. Instead of cultivating our wisdom we end up feeding our greed.

I am often in contact with people who are in the profession of helping those who are physically or mentally not well - these days, there are so many of them! Many of these professional people who are working eight or twelve hours a day, month after month, seem to breakdown quite easily, thinking, 'I'm serving all the time, I'm giving all the time and it's draining all my energy, it drains everything from me.' They feel they've been doing so much for others that they are completely worn out and have no energy left to look after themselves. But if you're like Mother Theresa, or other highly realised beings, helping others unconditionally actually gives you inner energy. I've been with some of these committed beings: they don't even miss sleep because there's so much commitment on their part, so much joy in what they're able to do to help! This feeling of tiredness, of losing energy disappears and there is instead an extraordinary inner joy. You feel so happy to have come to this world with this ability, this opportunity to help other beings. When you are able to do this, if your mind feels joyful by just being able to serve and look after others, it's as if the people you are helping are giving you the energy you need. You've nothing to lose. There is no 'me' who is working so hard and giving all the time, but there is joy.

Whatever you do, the way you see it is, in a way, more important than what you do. You need to always keep an open frame of mind. If you are working in a social or therapeutic field, I would advise you to meditate every morning and rejoice that you're not as sick as all these people who really need to be taken care of all the time. Rejoice that you're not in as bad a situation as they are, and that you have this wonderful opportunity to help them. If you're really able to think like that, you'll be stronger, more energetic than ever before. You will experience growing joy and happiness.

If we consider the issue from the point of view of the Buddhist philosophy, living this life is like acting in a drama. In reality, there isn't 'them' and there isn't 'me', so who is tired and who is helped? This is another way of looking at it. If 'I' don't exist, if 'they' don't exist, who do I think I'm helping? And who is the one thinking that they are tired? If this so-called 'me', this ego, doesn't exist, then who is tired? If we're able to see that we're just acting a kind of drama for the short time of this life, this will give us a feeling of energy and enthusiasm to be able to help others. I think some of this information is very, very useful.

People who feel unhappy search for care, sympathy, appreciation and love from others because they don't know how to find happiness within themselves, but as long as they search for it outside, they will never find complete and lasting satisfaction. Therefore, in meditation, one has to remember first to develop compassion and loving kindness towards oneself. If we

42

don't know how to be loving and kind towards ourselves in the first place, how can we be kind and loving towards others? Instead of leading a life full of hatred and unhappiness, we should always remember this loving kindness and develop Bodhicitta, the motivation to work for the benefit of all sentient beings.

Once we start to meditate, if we feel very inspired by the Bodhicitta motivation and get carried away by the idea, 'How wonderful! I am going to meditate in order to lead a very positive life and liberate all sentient beings' then we are still keeping our mind busy, which is a waste of time according to the Mahamudra teachings. Whether our thoughts are positive or negative is not the point. Both kinds disturb our meditation. We should just take the commitment in the beginning, and that is enough. It is like ploughing a field. If we plough the field properly and plant very pure seeds, we don't need to dig up the seeds all the time to see whether there is any result. We should know that, if we have done everything properly, there will be a pure fruition. As practitioners, all we need to do is meditate, without our mind engaging in anything.

A beginner's attitude

We should start by sitting in whatever position is most comfortable for us. Feeling physically comfortable will help us relax mentally and this is exactly what we should do: just sit completely relaxed physically and mentally. Our body is here and our mind is also here. If both are disconnected, what is the use of sitting here while our mind is rampaging all over the place? The whole purpose of sitting is to bring the mind back. This alone shows us that mind and body are not the same thing. If mind and body were one and the same, how could the body sit here and the mind be all over the place? The idea is not to complicate the practice. We are just simply sitting here quietly, calmly, peacefully, and our mind has no cause to complain, because we are asking nothing of it!

Meditation instructions always state that we should try to find the right environment in which to practise. When we learn to meditate, it may be easier to work on our frame of mind if we have less to complain about at the physical level. When we are sitting in a beautiful shrine room we have to admit that we are in the right place and have no reason to complain! However, all of us will go through different experiences. This shows us clearly that what we experience has much less to do with our environment than with our state of mind.

Beginners may discover that their mind is awfully busy. They may think that meditation is making it even worse than before and wonder whether meditation is appropriate for them. Actually, they simply discover all the 'busy-ness' that has been going on in their head all the time, which they hadn't noticed before. Traditionally, the beginner's mind is compared to a big waterfall. What happens is that when we start to sit, we get a glimpse of it! Meditation is not making our mind chaotic but rather makes us see how chaotic it currently is. This is how we are and we should not be afraid of such experiences.

For beginners, it is always very good to approach meditation with a very open mind. We should not start meditating with the wish to have a peaceful mind, very good experiences, and so on. If we expect certain experiences, we will just be watching for them to come and when things do not happen as we want, we will feel very dissatisfied.

To have a 'beginners' attitude' we should be open minded without expectations. We should sit in a quiet place with no distractions and give ourselves time to meditate, allowing our body and mind to relax and settle. Our body sits here and our mind stays with our body. In this way, whenever we see our mind jumping out of the room, we just kindly bring it back. It doesn't matter how many times we have to repeat this. If today we have to bring it back every second for half an hour of meditation, it is still worthwhile.

Things can go wrong when our worldly impatience starts to manifest. But getting upset destroys everything. We should be very patient and patience means never getting upset, never getting angry. Let's be happy and feel good that we can just be aware of our mind wandering away and remember to bring it back. If we think that our mind is too bad and if we get angry or feel miserable, we cannot make any progress.

Forgiveness

The past is what disturbs us most. To sit in meditation can bring up a lot of pain linked with past experiences. We want to forget them but the thoughts keep coming back. For instance, many people seem to have suffered because of their parents. Children expect a lot from their parents and when they are hurt, it becomes almost impossible for them to let go; they keep their painful memories alive. We should not be attached to our past experiences. Keeping them alive does not improve our situation, it actually makes things worse. If we are incapable of letting go of what has happened to us, it is as if a poisonous snake had bitten us and we are unable to get rid of the poison. We then lead a meaningless and very unhappy life because we refuse to forgive. Christianity as well as Buddhism always teaches us to forgive. If we can't forgive things that are giving us great pain and suffering, we have a big problem! Pain and suffering are there because we make such a big deal out of whatever happened in the past. We create a monster out of nothing.

Every practitioner should become wise and learn how to let go of the past by forgiving, by finding the reasons why we should learn to forgive. Some people think that they can't forgive because the pain they went through was too great. But what does keeping these memories actually do to them? Are other people still torturing them? Actually, they are allowing their mind to be poisoned. Their inability to forgive is not improving their situation but making it worse.

Usually, those who are the objects of such strong

and long lasting grudges are precisely those who have been dearest to us. We have built a relationship based on trust and big expectations, and when things went wrong, we felt deeply hurt, which reveals our ignorant side. If we were really wise, we wouldn't have made these people so important in the first place.

There are many ways to learn how to forgive, but it can only really be achieved through meditation. If we don't meditate, we do not reach such a conclusion in the first place: we just run away from our own shadow. When we meditate, we see why our life is unsatisfactory, why we are suffering. We should go back to the very source of that chaos, pin it down and find ways and means to forgive. Through meditation, we can develop the wish to change, to let go of the pain coming from the past, and only then can we really change. When we are able to achieve this, I assure you that our whole life becomes meaningful. It is like finally putting down a heavy weight we have been carrying for so many years. Many people may think it is impossible to forgive, so let me give you the example of my own life.

I was fourteen when I escaped from Tibet. The Chinese communists' main aim was to make everyone think their way. They soon realised that the Tibetans had great devotion to the Lamas, so the Lamas became a target. We fled our monastery and were walking by night for fear of being caught by day. Our escape lasted many months and was very hard. Our group numbered about three hundred people who had left everything, all their worldly possessions behind. We were trying to cross mountains in very cold weather with no proper food, no proper sleep and in constant fear of being caught. We had heard how the Chinese soldiers killed and tortured those they caught. Our aim was to reach Lhasa where we thought we would be safe, but we found out that Lhasa had already been taken over. We then had to cross the Brahmaputra, which is a very big, powerful river. The only way to cross it was to make a coracle. We camped up in the mountain and built a kind of box made of leather. We collected pine resin that we melted and pasted on the leather to prevent water from getting through.

Our dinghy could only carry four or five people and out of our group, only one person knew how to row! Tibetans are not used to crossing big rivers with boats! One Rinpoche looked with binoculars to find a place were it would be safe to cross, because many soldiers were posted by the riverbanks. But somehow, the scenery at night was quite different from what it looked like by day. We intended to cross several times to fetch everybody but on the first trip, the boat with my brother and I on board had not even reached the other bank when the soldiers started to shoot.

At first, I was not aware of what was going on. An old Lama who was with us told us the Chinese were there. He had many relics that he put around my neck and holding my arm, he took me with him. We had to jump into the water and splash our way to the other side. We were wearing sheepskin coats, but it was the middle of winter and the water was icy cold. As soon as we came out of the water, the coats were completely frozen. We hid under big tree trunks and dared not come out. The soldiers were there, going up and down, we heard them moving all around us.

From then onwards, I had terrible nightmares almost every night. We were running away with the soldiers chasing us, we were almost caught and each time I experienced this terrible fear surging up.

When I became a monk, my teacher told me that I had to learn to forgive, otherwise this pain would never go away. During my first five years of solitary retreat in the state of New York, I diligently applied what we call the practise of the 'Four Foundations' in which one invites all the beings one considers as one's enemies and leads them on the right path. I started by wondering who was responsible for bringing so much suffering to my family and all the Tibetans. I figured out that not every Chinese was responsible for it, as the Chinese people also suffered a lot under that regime. I decided that Mao Tze Tong and his Prime Minister must be responsible, so I invited them to come close to me and tried to make friends with them.

After three years, one night I had a wonderful dream. I was opening a nice medium sized grocery store, selling food and fruits, and both of them were my attendants, helping me do my business. From then onwards, my nightmares were gone! Now I am able to have many good Chinese friends.

I'm not talking about what Christ or the Buddha accomplished, but about the forgiveness that any human being can achieve. This is my experience. People often think that Lamas are somehow different, but twenty years ago, I was worse than any one of you. Most of you are, in many ways, in a better state than I was. However I managed to deal with my problems because I wholeheartedly believed that this path was the right one if I wished to let go of my pain and suffering.

People suffer because of what happened in their past and because they think it is unforgivable, but there is nothing unforgivable. It is like a very heavy, painful load we carry with us all our life, but we can put it down. When the pain comes up, when the emotions become so strong, so real, so powerful, we should learn how to put a gentle stop to them. It's past, finished, gone!

This attachment to the past is also linked to most Westerners' problem with guilt. I think this so-called 'guilty business' is a product of your upbringing. Your culture and religion can make you feel guilty. In Tibetan Buddhism, we don't allow ourselves to feel guilty and just do nothing to make things better. If I find that I'm on the wrong side, I have to do everything to go back to the right side. Feeling guilty doesn't help, hating yourself because you feel you are so horrible, feeling bad and miserable, this sort of attitude doesn't do you or anybody any good.

The Buddhist approach means that when I see I've done something wrong, I do prostrations and ask for forgiveness. It's like when I've fallen in the mud, my clothes are dirty, so I take a bath and I put my clothes in the laundry. They come out dry and clean: that's the Vajrayana practice! If you've fallen in the mud, you wouldn't leave this mud on you all your life. You would be stinking! This is where the difference comes. After the bath, you feel really good. You accepted your wrong points, you made things right and you are now a better, more positive human being. Don't ever sleep on your guilty feelings, because it will make you stink! If you don't want to do anything to correct the situation, why do you keep that guilt anyway? If you find out you've done something terribly wrong, you should really do all you can to repair it and make things right and then it's your duty to get over feelings of guilt.

Sometimes, I feel really sorry for you all, because when talking about meditation, I'm teaching you exactly the opposite of what you were brought up to think. For instance, if I say to you not to follow the past, people may have difficulties accepting the idea. If you go to a psychiatrist, you are urged not to suppress your past but to bring it back, to talk and talk about it or to write it down. This makes you feel that your past experiences and the sufferings connected to them are really true. But we Buddhists say that ego doesn't exist in the first place, therefore how can the problems themselves actually exist? I am not suggesting that one should deny one's past, that is impossible anyway. To deny means that one first accepts there is something to be denied! What I am saying is that there is nothing to be denied, nothing to be suppressed.

Therefore, in meditation, when a thought or an emotion arises, our 'number one' duty is not to follow it, not to feed it, but also not to deny it. If that thought disrupts our meditation a thousand times, we should be patient, tolerant, and never get upset. When we have learnt how to leave it alone, this strong wave of energy will gradually subside. If, on the contrary, we consider that we are strong enough to suppress the thought or emotion, we will only give it greater strength and we will never be able to really suppress it because there is actually nothing to suppress.

Of course, we shouldn't forget our past mistakes if we don't want to repeat them in the future, but we should not let our past experiences ruin our life. To draw lessons from the past has some relevance but to keep alive past sufferings is very wrong because it hurts us, harms others and doesn't solve any problems.

I have been talking about suffering linked to past experiences, but some people may have had wonderful experiences in the past. However, if they go back to them, they are not going to find inner peace either. We are meditating in order to try to perfect our Buddha nature. Good thoughts or bad thoughts make no difference, both mean wasting our time. If we let ourselves be drawn into the happiness of positive ideas or the unhappiness of negative ones, we will constantly swing from one state to the other. We should get rid of this. The Buddhist approach is to rub the one against the other, like two pieces of wood: when they ignite, the fire consumes both, nothing is left, no negative, no positive, no right or wrong. To achieve some realisation means to reach a state of mind in which all is the same because we have perfect control over our mind, our speech and our physical actions.

Not engaging in the past

The thoughts, emotions and feelings that come should not be rejected or suppressed: we should simply leave them alone. If our mind keeps on rebelling and fighting, we may ask ourselves whether we are human beings or monkeys. Monkeys have to be entertained all the time. They are constantly looking for excitement and trying to experiment with everything. We are supposed to be human beings, able to think and to stop thinking at will. We thus discover that, contrary to what we usually believe, we do not control our mind. We have to learn this control.

What Mahamudra requires is just that our mind be where our body is. If the mind is here, the first point is that it should not follow the past. For all of us, pain and pleasure, good and bad experiences all start in the past. When people are meditating, their mind is always engaging in thoughts. All these thoughts, when we let them happen, are just never-ending! There is no limit to their number and variety, and they will keep us so busy that we will never find any calm. However, if we just leave them alone, not denying but also not following these feelings, emotions and thoughts of right and wrong, then past sufferings, pain and bad experiences will no longer torment us during the meditation because we have decided that we will no longer let them bother us. We may currently have domestic or professional problems and, when we meditate, these problems catch up with us. Whenever this happens, we should remember the idea of 'non-grasping'. We are giving ourselves some time to meditate and we should not allow problems to interfere with our meditation.

We have been brought up to believe that we should use every moment to solve our problems, but very often, thinking about problems doesn't solve them and only generates more anxiety. For the time we dedicate to meditation, we should gently put a stop to our usual 'problem solving' and leave our worries alone. Of course, all kinds of thoughts will start coming. If our thoughts are connected to the past, we shouldn't follow them. We shouldn't let ourselves be tortured by our own old habits. If we let our mind go back to the past, it means never-ending suffering.

Not engaging in the future

Now that we have somehow managed not to engage in the past, our mind doesn't know what to do. It gets bored because it is used to being very busy and, maybe after a few seconds or a few minutes, we start thinking of the future. Thoughts and emotions linked to the future are also limitless. You have always been told to plan everything, to think ahead, and I'm now telling you not to think, not to plan! That is again completely the opposite to what you may have been taught. Indeed, according to Buddhism, it is not our planning or our thinking that makes things happen and work for us, but it is our karma. The future is like a huge hurricane that just sweeps us along. Whatever was meant to happen is what happens. How many plans have we made in our life and how many worked out? If we examine it carefully, we will see that hardly any of them worked out as planned! What benefit did our planning bring? It was a total waste of time.

If planning was the only way for us to achieve the wished for results, this whole modern civilisation should be a perfect place. But it doesn't seem to be the case. Our families had a plan for us. As soon as we were born, they wanted us to become doctors or lawyers. Parents always have great plans for their children. We had our own aspirations, which we tried to make happen, but sometimes our plans never even took off. Some people will spend four or five years of their life studying something to get a good degree and afterwards discover it is not what they wanted to do, or they do not get a job and their degree becomes useless. If I take myself as an example, I never thought I would become a Lama and teach. It just happened. I wanted to meditate and do retreat - for the rest of my life. I felt so lucky not to be missing food, partners or anything... but I was given no choice. I didn't plan to become a teacher and yet it happened. Other people may really want to teach and yet it doesn't happen. Therefore we shouldn't spend too much time planning our lives, and especially not when we are supposed to be meditating. The main point in meditating is to achieve some clarity. Then we will automatically do what is right in our lives.

Agitation and torpor

Let us now consider the two main obstacles to meditation. The first is agitation. When you try to meditate, you have so much energy that your mind gets very chaotic and you cannot sit properly and meditate. Your mind is very busy and all over the place. If that happens to you, instead of getting irritated, you should relax physically and mentally. Don't worry too much about the proper sitting posture, but relax deep inside like people do when they want to go to sleep; try to feel heavy, look downward to the ground as if you were trying to pull the energy down. It will ground you.

The second obstacle occurs when you feel quiet and peaceful but very sleepy. According to Buddhism, sleep is an ignorant state of mind because during sleep you don't produce any positive result. Moreover, it is a major obstacle to meditation. When you feel sleepy, check your posture and correct it, sit up and look upward. This will wake you up. Sometimes it can also happen that when we experience some peace in the mind, we prefer not to wake up and, in a way, create sleep. We are often too easily satisfied and prefer to enjoy sleep rather than experience our usual ongoing mental chaos. We should definitely not be afraid of our chaotic mind. We should keep our mind peaceful but awake. Sharpening our motivation will help us. We haven't come here to sleep. We already spend half of our life sleeping!

In Vajrayana, torpor is considered as a negative energy and we use purification techniques to get rid of too much sleepiness. When we do a lot of purification, sleep is less necessary. Milarepa did not need sleep. He had reached a state of mind in which sleep is no longer a requirement.

Any meditator will sometimes encounter agitation or torpor, but if one can remember to apply the right antidote, one will be able to overcome these two major obstacles, namely a mind either too busy to settle down or too sleepy to meditate.

Impermanence

Everything is so impermanent. A good practitioner does not even think about what to do tomorrow, knowing that one might not even be alive. In this modern civilisation, people don't like to think about impermanence and death because it is too painful, but everybody is actually confronted with impermanence constantly. Impermanence is experienced by everybody, at every moment of every day. One minute you'll see wonderful weather, the sun shining, the sky all blue, and the next minute, the sun is gone, it's cold and windy. Everything in this world changes. Our relationships keep on changing. Our own inner feelings and our mind also keep changing all the time. There is nothing in our whole experience that can be labelled 'forever'.

If our state of mind keeps on changing, if nothing remains forever, a wise person will wonder why we pursue things that we know we are going to lose eventually. It's only a matter of time, somehow we are going to lose whatever we have.

My own life is an illustration of the nature of impermanence. In Tibet we were monks, we had everything, we were important, and the next day we were nobody, we didn't even have a cup to drink water from. And now again, we are 'somebody'. Tomorrow, somehow, we may be nobody again. People who have everything may one day have nothing and people who have nothing now may one day have something. That's called the nature of impermanence. Everything can change. It keeps on changing. Wise people have no doubt about this.

Some people feel that thinking about

impermanence is painful. However, if we face up to impermanence, it will be much easier to handle when we actually experience it. There are schools of thought that say your entire life should be excitement, enjoyment and happiness - and of course who wouldn't like to have such a life?

Buddha isn't denying this. Sometimes people say, 'We don't like Buddhism because this constant thinking about impermanence, death and suffering is so painful! It makes us suffer more'. This is so unwise. How could the Buddha's intention ever be to increase our sufferings? The Buddha only wished to free us from suffering.

We are sometimes so naïve. We don't really want to acknowledge impermanence. We hide and totally deny our age, but that's very foolish. Even if we don't want to age, wrinkles keep on coming. We're going to get older every day. Look at my head now. Youth is gone. We need to really take it easy and enjoy it. We have to be joyful that we're ageing! Age is something that starts as soon as we are born. Which philosophy would deny this?

Some people also think that now that they are young, they have to enjoy life and that they have no time for practice. They think they will have the opportunity to practise when they're older. According to the Buddha's teachings, impermanence means that death doesn't wait for someone to grow old, it can happen at any time to anybody. A young child born yesterday may die today. Many young people die at the very best time of their life.

Death can come in so many ways. We drive in a car and have an accident... We think that food is a substance that is giving us life, maintaining our life form. But sometimes the food we eat poisons us and kills us.... There are so many ways of dying. That is also a sign of impermanence. Therefore we can't really just wait until we get old before we practice.

Impermanence is everywhere at every level. If we're wise, we won't have any doubt about it. Therefore, if everything is impermanent, we see clearly that there is no need to plan ahead and spend too much time thinking about what we will do in the future. The days, months and years of our lives are passing so fast. By the time we think we have achieved something, it is too late because we are too old to enjoy it. We should understand the nature of impermanence and see that tomorrow may be too late to start practising. We could be dead! We all have different karmas, so it's better to do something while we can.

Refusing to think about impermanence means denying the realities of life. Denying reality is useless. You know deep down in your mind that you will get old. You know deep down in your mind, you will die one day. Nobody can actually guarantee that you will be alive tomorrow. Good practitioners are not even supposed to think about tomorrow. All they want is to make this very minute as meaningful as possible because they are aware that whatever happens tomorrow will be tomorrow and they might no longer be alive. We can plan everything we like, but we can't deny reality, which has the nature of impermanence.

What does Buddhism say about the nature of impermanence? Look at a house for instance. It seems to you very solid, you can see it, but isn't it also like a vision in somebody's head? Some hundred years ago, the house was not there, and also it doesn't remain forever. It's like the movies you watch on television: many things happen but it's all fiction, these people are acting and you know nothing is truly happening. What's the difference with our lives? In fact it's exactly the same. You are looking at people's lives, you're looking at all these seemingly solid forms, but they are all changing and impermanent. The best way to understand what the Buddha said about 'emptiness' is to reflect on and find out about the nature of impermanence.

The word 'emptiness' is used in English because we had no alternative but to use it. Unfortunately, the minute we say 'emptiness', people get very, very lost. They think it's like something empty, hollow, like throwing a stone in the ocean - it gets lost, you have no clue as to where the stone has gone. So they refuse to hear what the Buddha is saying because they think that if life is like this, it will only double up their sufferings. This is a misunderstanding. When the Buddha talks about emptiness, he's saying that nothing ever remains the same. Wherever you look, you will find impermanence. Even that which seems biggest and most solid hasn't been there forever and will not be there forever in the future. When we realise that everything is impermanent, we understand that we have no time to waste and that what we really need is to have enough wisdom to invest our time and energy into the right direction, with the right objective.

For instance, sometimes people think that their relationship will last forever - or at least for the rest of their life. If something like a relationship could work in this world, the West should be the best place for such lasting relationships to take place, because you have all the time to pursue and choose your partner, to really get to know each other. But if I take a look at what's really happening, I can only come to the conclusion that, either you're very bad choosers or there's no permanence! Few people seem to stay together. Why is it that, with the choice you have, with all the effort you put into the process, your relationship doesn't last when you've finally found a partner? It is because your mind keeps on changing. When you want something, nothing can stop you from having it. You become so positive! So tolerant! If there is some person you want badly, even if he or she is the worst person one can think of, you still view him or her as some sort of god or goddess. You're so good at building up such an image. This person can do nothing wrong. Everything is positive. You admire everything. It doesn't matter if he or she's kicking somebody, you still think it's wonderful!

But once you get the person, you start discovering faults. You first made a long list of this person's wonderful qualities: nothing was wrong, everything 100% perfect. But now that you can say, 'He or she is mine', you start noticing one defect after another and listing what's wrong with this person. And your wonderful life is gone with this! If your mind was unchangeable, things like this wouldn't happen.

The little bit of time you might be able to find for meditation can help you become wiser. You can really take the time to think all this over. You can try to kid other people by telling them you're having a wonderful time, but if you're actually having an awful time, you can't kid yourself. In meditation, you need to go through this, and in the process you'll become wiser. If you're really a stable, wise person, before getting involved in anything, you will investigate whether it's really useful. Is this something worthwhile? Is it really going to benefit me for a long time? Or is it something I can waste many years pursuing and then the minute I find it, I lose it?

When you are practising, you can really understand the changeable nature of everything. If you are wise, you should then value all of these things less because you know it doesn't matter how much energy you put into getting them, it doesn't matter how much you value them, somehow they're not going to last.

But then thinking about this, some people, instead of making the right move so their life becomes more meaningful, fall into sadness, wondering what they're doing on earth and thinking their life has no meaning, no value any more. That's not true! We came here for very good reasons. We are human beings, we are intelligent. We came into this world to free ourselves forever. Ours isn't a hopeless case. We should see that this reflection on impermanence is all about becoming truly free. That's the truth. We all want to be free.

We should be thinking, 'How can I free myself? Because the greater my freedom and stability, the more I will be able to help others.' The more unstable we are, the more negative we become. The more insecure we are, the more we distort reality and project our own inner insecurity onto people and situations around us. Lacking the right view, we contribute to the world's sufferings because without the right view we can't have the right conduct. Therefore, meditation not only genuinely helps us to become better human beings but also, through achieving this goal benefits everybody. I think we will be more generous if we don't have a strong grasping mind, if we don't feel strong desire and attachment. Then everything we do will be more pure and beneficial.

The whole purpose of Buddha's teaching about impermanence is for us to give less value to things that are never going to last, so that we invest less effort into those things and use all our time and energy for the benefit of others. Everything is really about learning to become wiser, better human beings.

We eat the best food, we take so much care of our body with washing, cleaning and clothing, but why is our mind so unsteady, so emotional, so weak? We have never given it proper care; our mind has never been given one minute of rest. It is just constantly abused. When we put too much pressure on our mind, it is very likely that it will have a disastrous effect on our body and cause it to fall sick. Therefore the whole purpose of meditation is to look into other ways and means of finding fulfilment and satisfaction, and the fruition of practising is that after some time we become kinder and gentler.

We usually believe that we have to think, that thinking is the only way to solve our problems, but in fact we completely waste our mental energy. What we really need to understand is that the moment we let our mind rest is the first time we give ourselves some space. You should therefore never feel guilty of 'doing nothing' when you are giving yourself twenty or thirty minutes to meditate. If being busy were going to bring you all you need, you would already have it, as you have already been scheming and planning all of your life! For the time of your meditation, your mind doesn't need to engage in any planning.

If our thoughts are not engaging in the past and not engaging in the future, then we are where we want to be. We should therefore be totally relaxed. Unfortunately, once we manage this, then our mind really starts to get upset. We can't stay content because our mind is so used to thinking and doing something. Now we don't know what to do without any thoughts. If I were to give you real Mahamudra meditation instructions, I would only tell you: ' Don't speak, don't think, don't meditate, just sit.' But I have great sympathy for you all and I don't think beginners can observe such instructions.

As I previously remarked, Westerners have all been brought up in a culture that sets busy-ness and activity as a model. You are convinced that you have to do many things and keep your minds busy in order to find a meaning in life. You are busy thinking all the time. Then I tell you to sit and not to think. Instead of finding a calm and peaceful mind, you discover a tricky, changeable, chaotic mind. Your mind has been so busy for so long! You sit for a while and finally find some calm, but you are so convinced that you should be constantly working hard that you then think, 'I'm wasting my time doing nothing!' That is your first thought. But that is totally wrong! You have already wasted all your life thinking and messing around! This is the first time you are actually developing some wisdom.

Wisdom

A mind that is thinking too much is like very agitated water, where all the mud and dirt has been stirred up from the bottom. If one allows the water to become calm and still, the mud will sink to the bottom, and the water becomes clear and clean. If the water is clear, one can see through it and drink it. A calm mind is like pure clear water - all the disturbing thoughts have settled. We will be able to achieve everything without too much thinking. With stability, calmness and wisdom, everything becomes easy. Too much thinking, a lack of stability and wisdom is like having no eyes; we are busy trying to walk among people, pushing everybody and finally we fall over! Therefore we should never allow ourselves to get into the idea that meditating and thinking nothing is a waste of time. Letting go of the pressure to think all the time is the most precious, wonderful and profound thing we can ever do.

Wisdom is absolutely necessary in every aspect of life. Every one of us needs wisdom. Some people tell me that so and so has such a great knowledge in so many fields, that he's so wise, but I think that they mistake simple knowledge for wisdom. Nowadays all children go to school and learn things. Knowledge is not a problem. People know more than is actually necessary. But if you don't have wisdom, this knowledge is more or less useless. Your head is full of information, but you don't know how to use it all correctly. That's why wisdom is essential.

In ancient civilisations, older people were respected for their wisdom. Wise people never do anything without first thinking about the consequences of their actions and they always have a good reason for doing whatever they do in life. A wise person knows before speaking whether his or her speech is useful or not, whether it's necessary or not. Before doing anything in their lives, they first evaluate whether there's an overall benefit rather than a selfish one. Unwise people never ever bring other beings into their frame of thoughts. Every decision they take is focused on 'me'. 'What's in it for me?' Everything is based on their own needs, their own wants. They are so self-oriented that they can never make an impartial decision from which everybody can benefit. A decision from which 90% of the people involved will benefit is a good decision taken with wisdom, but if it only benefits you and nobody else, it is a very selfish decision taken without wisdom.

The first step to develop wisdom is to start to see that this present life we have as human beings is a very, very precious one. Buddhists say that this human life is as rare as a star visible during the day. Stars are always there but due to the bright daylight, we don't see them. To attain a human life is the very best condition one can ever achieve. If we understand this fully, we will want to make the best of this precious opportunity and not misuse it through lack of wisdom.

Gaining more wisdom, becoming a wise human being, means that, before engaging in something, you will consider whether it is going to be useful for you. 'Should I really invest so many years, so much money and so much effort trying to get all this? What real benefit will it bring for me and for mankind?' In this way, if you have a calm and clear mind, then every decision is made with wisdom and you can improve the situation all the time.

Wisdom helps you to gauge a situation and take the right decision. We find good examples in the Buddha's teachings. Suppose someone is an ignorant, evil person doing great harm in the world and causing much suffering. Then it would be our duty to do what we can to prevent this person from harming others and creating bad karma for themselves. We should act with wisdom arising from our Bodhisattva motivation to protect life and prevent suffering. Our motivation is, first of all, to save this misguided human being from doing wrong actions that would have terrible results for himself. At the same time we want to save all the people who would suffer due to this person's actions. If we are rigid, if we have no flexibility, no wisdom, we will think, 'Oh, I've taken vows. It doesn't matter whether that person is making such an awful mistake, I cannot interfere.' And we will close our eyes. But vows are also flexible. In a way whatever we do with selfish interests is a real violation of our vows.

I think we need wisdom for everything we do in our everyday life. For instance, we can investigate whether we should really invest so much time and energy in running after a partner and relationships. You can easily see how long it takes to build up a relationship. And once you succeed, how sensitive you have to be all the time not to upset your friend. Nevertheless, in the end, one day it's gone all the same! None of your hard work has achieved anything and you've been suffering all the time. You were walking on a knife's edge all the time and then you fell down and cut yourself.

I am puzzled by what you call 'free relationships' in the West! If that were really to work for you, you should also be free from emotions and free from attachment! It's very good, it seems to be so excellent to have relationships with anybody whom you want, but if you really want to be free, then you should be free from any strong attachment because attachment goes together with suffering and pain.

But somehow everything seems to be upside-down. It's as if at the same time you're saying 'free', you are also saying you should have the strongest attachment and desire, and the most grasping mind. What I can see is that nobody's free! You're all so much involved at the deepest level with clinging, with holding on, wrapping it all up in jealousy...

If you were really free, you should be like birds. Birds can fly wherever they want and land wherever they want. But with your so-called 'freedom', you try to catch a bird and the minute you get it, you want to imprison it by putting it in the cage of your jealousy. That's the only way you think you can keep your relationship going, but jealousy and the happiness you want are totally opposite. I think that most of the time you get more pain and suffering having such relationships than if you hadn't any. Losing, gaining, it's here, it's gone, oh, where is it? This keeps on going, keeps on coming, year after year, never ending. It's ongoing suffering.

To be really 'free' means, you either don't need to have a relationship, so you're completely free, or if you want to have many, you don't have any strong attachment. You want to have a kind of god-like lifestyle - nothing but pleasures, excitement, happiness and joy. But if everything in your life is mixed up with all the poisons, with jealousy, anger, attachment, then in return you'll get nothing but more and more suffering. We always need to remember that whenever we think of freedom, nobody can give us this freedom; we can only free ourselves. This means we should free ourselves from desire and attachment. If we are able to do this, then we are totally free. As long as we have these needs and wants, we can't call ourselves free.

According to the Mahamudra tradition, we say 'No hope, no fear!' This means that if you really want to be free, you should have no need to have such a relationship. If there is no hope, there will never be any fear of not getting what you want or losing what you have got. Fear comes with hope. The minute you're hoping for something, fear pops up: fear of not getting it. The minute you get something, fear is there, the fear of losing it. Between these two, hope and fear, we keep on suffering all the time.

Linked to relationships, I also think an area where wisdom would be very useful, is having and raising children. So many women and girls in Europe think that just because they are females, they must have children. But why? You shouldn't have children unless you can pass on to them what I would call a 'good lineage.' I'm passing on to you a spiritual lineage, but family lineages are also important. A child who has been abused will blame his or her parents for it all their life. There's no need to have something to show in order to prove that you're a woman. You don't have to have a child because everybody else is having children, or because everybody is expecting you to have one. That doesn't make any sense. If you have wisdom, you should instead think, 'I don't have to have a child because society says so. What can I actually offer to this child?' You need to have a child only when you are willing to commit yourself to being the best mother. If this isn't the case, why should you have children who are going to suffer all the time because you brought them into your life just to have a toy to play with? A child is not a toy, it's a human being! Children need loving kindness and caring, all the time, day and night. I don't have to tell you, all of you know that caring for children requires lots of time and energy. But if you already have to work so hard, if you're already fully stressed, will you be able to give your child the loving care it needs? If you can't look after your children very well, they child will suffer all their lives.

I'm telling you this because I think it may help many people. I have met so many children from wealthy families, who have said to me: 'I don't care for what they give me. Money means nothing to me! If I don't get any love and kindness from my parents, they can keep their money, what's the good of it?' If you don't take the time to care for your children and love them, and if you tell them instead that you're working very hard to make money so that you can leave them something later, do you think they're really going to appreciate this?

When we're grown up, we're capable of looking after ourselves, but being a child means complete dependence on our parents for everything. If you let someone down at the time of childhood, from then onwards this person will lack self-confidence. Such people will find it impossible to trust anybody because when they needed it most, their strongest expectation was never fulfilled and they never learned to trust.

Nowadays, in Europe feeding a family is not a problem. But you need peace of mind. You need to give a child a foundation, some sort of stability, so that he or she will have a direction and grow up with the ability to survive in this world. Otherwise, everybody in the family will suffer. And the parents will be given the hardest time when these children grow up.

So many families are not prepared. Many people take commitments that they can't even stick to for six months! But making a commitment to a family is for more than twenty one years, until the child is a self-sufficient adult. Therefore you should ask yourself, 'Do I have the wisdom, do I have the strength, to really commit myself for this length of time?'

If you really think you need to have someone to look after, there are millions of children starving to death. You can give them money and they will be so grateful. Your own children will often take everything you give for granted. They'll have no gratitude because they think it's their right and there's no need to thank you for that. But if you give even half a pound to someone else's babies, they're very grateful.

Many decent families do everything to bring up their children properly. They teach them not to smoke, not to do this, not to do that. They succeed until the child goes to school. Then they come in contact with other children who tell them, 'You're weird. You don't fit in You'd better take some grass!' And that's the end of their discipline.

What's the use of putting so much effort into bringing up your children properly if it's all wasted as soon as you send them to school? Nowadays young boys and girls think that they are weird if they don't smoke or copy what other people do. It's something fashionable and young people trying not to smoke are isolated. Having fewer and fewer friends, one day they join the pack, and as they were denied doing all this when they were young, they now think, 'I'm free, really it's wonderful, yes!'

We need wisdom to help those school children, to show them there are many other ways of enjoying life. Especially nowadays, you can show them the wonders of the natural world and take them to the countryside, teach them to be healthy human beings instead of damaging their health with smoke or abuse of alcohol, or taking all types of wonder drugs. Seeing all this, I feel very sorry for all the people who put so much effort into bringing up their children the right way and yet fail completely.

These days, bringing up children is so difficult because there seem to be so many obstacles everywhere. That's why it is better to avoid the responsibility of having children, if you don't feel really prepared to face the challenge. We always say that we should maintain the level of our population but why should we have too many people to feed? If in the end there are fewer people but they are all decent human beings, then there's no problem. But nowadays, it seems that decent human beings are getting fewer every day!

First of all, this is because people don't have the time to gain inner wisdom. If we leave our mind the way it is, it can give us lots of chaos. An untamed mind is a very complicated mind. For instance, you think you need someone but if that person pays attention to you, you feel no interest because it's too easy, whereas if somebody rejects you, you'll be willing to kill yourself chasing after this person, thinking, 'I must get him or her!'

Why do we have to make our lives so complicated and think everything has to be difficult if we want to get any satisfaction?

If we don't allow ourselves to follow a spiritual path, everything we do will be to satisfy our worldly ambitions, our worldly goals, which have no certainty. I think the wealthy people in the world may now have more pain and suffering, worrying about their money, than those people who sleep in the street. Beggars have much less to worry about. When people who don't have much think they'd be happier if they had more wealth, I think they are totally wrong. We have to be more realistic. Happiness doesn't come from wealth or from relationships.

Having wisdom means you should be really honest with yourself when you look at situations. If you were to put as much energy into your meditation as you put into pursuing worldly pleasures, I assure you, you would be a much happier person. I only say all this for your own benefit. If I don't pinpoint this, you may not even think about it. You think your lifestyle is perfect, because this is your tradition, this is your culture. As an outsider, I see things differently and I may be the right person to show you that another approach is possible.

In this way, whatever you do in your life, you always need wisdom in order to make the right decisions. I personally think it doesn't matter how old or how young you are, if you're always able to take the right decision by thinking before doing something instead of jumping into the action and reacting without thinking. And if you meditate regularly, then understanding comes. You will know what's right, what's wrong, what's good. Even when somebody makes you angry, before shouting back, you will think it over: 'Why did I actually let this person's words or actions upset me? Is it right to think I should fight back? And if I can just drop it, wouldn't everything be solved?'

In most cases and whatever level of emotion you're going through, if you meditate for a while, you can dissolve all these problems within the meditation. Maybe you don't need to do anything. Maybe you don't need to say anything. And even if you find that something really needs to be done, you'll find a way to deal wisely with that problem. Buddhists always talk about the need to combine 'method' and 'wisdom', to use skilful means. If you don't have wisdom, you can't have skilful means and ways of dealing with situations. People who lack wisdom never think about what they say and in this way they cause many problems. If you are skilful, you will know what is needed in order to help others You will always be very careful about what you say, so as not to hurt other people.

Meditation is the only way to fulfil our needs because, whatever we do in life, any decision, whether small or big, needs to be examined carefully. We need to see what is possible and what is not, what is necessary and what is not. Once we can sort that out, decision making becomes much easier.

Meditation is the right way to develop such skills and in order to do simple meditation, you don't have to go to temples, you don't have to become monks or nuns or Lamas, you can be whoever you are and just meditate whenever you find time. Regular practice will sharpen your awareness.

As I explained before, most of the time we forget where our mind has been going, we have no recollection, our mind just gets lost. Developing awareness means that you're aware of what you're saying, what you're eating, what you're thinking, and that awareness safeguards you from getting into any major difficulty. Lack of mindfulness is the reason why so many people make mistakes. According to Buddhism, if we are truly mindful, our pure Buddha nature will manifest and our actions will always be skilful. But through not having proper guidance and lacking awareness, people make mistakes.

Meditation means sharpening our awareness. We first learn this in formal sitting meditation and then learn to bring the same ability of mindfulness into ordinary life, even when we're not meditating in our room. Somehow this awareness must be present in our lives all the time, everywhere. Of course this is a gradual process and we first have to settle the mind.

Letting the mind settle

As I said, a beginner's mind is often compared to a big waterfall with thoughts tumbling down like rushing water, but there's no need to get upset or frustrated. Through regular practice it will gradually settle, become as gentle as a quiet river, and finally as deep and peaceful as an ocean without waves.

We shouldn't get impatient or angry if our mind keeps wandering and we have to bring it back every second. Anyway, mind cannot be subdued by anger; it can only be tamed with love and kindness. We should not, in the name of meditation, punish or upset ourselves. We should treat our mind the way a very tolerant and loving mother would treat her naughty child. The child has so much energy that it jumps and messes around all the time and tries to run out of the room. The mother doesn't get upset or angry, she doesn't beat it up. She lets it play, but within the confines of one room. Slowly, the naughty child will use up all his or her energy and come to rest. We should also allow our mind to jump anywhere it wants to jump, but watch it constantly and bring it back every time, a million times if necessary. We should not be judgmental, get impatient, discouraged or angry, otherwise our meditation will become very tense, difficult and painful. We give total space to our mind and let it wear out its own energy.

If we experience the 'big waterfall' and cannot control our mind, some breathing exercises might be quite good. Breathing is part of us. If you are a beginner you can close your eyes and use mental counting. With each in and out breath you count one. You count up to five, then start from the beginning again. We completely engage our mental activity in the breathing without thinking about anything else.

As we are now really trying to discipline our mind, it may react and reject it. If we try hard, we will become very tense and start complaining about headaches. Headaches come because we are getting too uptight. Mind has been able to do whatever it wanted for so long and now we are telling it to stay here quietly, so it gets angry.

If you start to get uptight while counting, stop counting and instead discuss with your mind: 'OK, now, I'm asking you nothing, so you have no good reason to complain.' We can discuss like this because we are talking all the time in our head in much the same way, and we really have to find ways and means to make our mind understand why we are doing what we are doing.

Sometimes people want a lot of information and, accordingly, Lamas give them a lot of information, but I think this may create obstacles. If people asked less, I would give them less information and they would have a simple meditation. This would be the best. As far as Mahamudra is concerned, the great Indian Master Tilopa put it very simply: 'Don't speak, don't think, don't meditate!' So simple! I am following this tradition but find myself giving students a hundred different methods! Students meditate and then come to me, 'Lama Yeshe, this breathing technique is not working for me, it's giving me a hard time.' I then explain to them how to focus on an object. Then they look at it and it gets strange, changing form and colour.

If we become very rigid in our meditation or put too much effort into it, we will get these kinds of hallucinations. When this happens, we should stop focusing on the object and just relax. We should apply effort very gently. So, when this happens, they come to me again and say 'Lama Yeshe, this is driving me crazy, please give me another method.' And I give them something else.

This is why we live in a world of abundant methods - because there are abundant needs and wants. People keep asking me for different methods and I keep giving them what they ask for, because that's the only way we can have some communication going on, but in the end, the same people complain, 'I don't like Tibetan Buddhism because it is so complicated. Why do we have to do all this?' But I never asked them to do all this. I always taught them how to be simple. I told them from the very beginning that it must be simple.

So, to start with, make no complications, just sit at ease, completely relaxed physically and mentally. Do not engage in past or future, do not even count your breathing. Just do nothing!

Confronting obstacles

When thoughts and emotions come, the more we push them away, the stronger they become. Sometimes, a particular thought or emotion may really bother us and we don't know how to get rid of it. Therefore we should try this time to introduce ourselves to our strongest, our number one emotional obstacle, be it anger, jealousy, attachment or whatever. We will confront it and, in order to do this, I will give you a specific meditation technique.

You should focus your mind diligently on an object such as a pebble or a Buddha statue, not allowing your mind to jump anywhere. Keep it connected to this object, which is like a pole. When you have a horse running everywhere, you put a rope around its neck and tie it to a pole. The horse can run around but not run away. The object is the pole, your awareness is the rope which ties you there. You're just watching this object and you're not letting your mind jump out anywhere.

You will notice small, insignificant distractions, subtle thoughts that appear and then dissolve. They are not a major problem, but if you stay for twenty four hours, they will get stronger and stronger. Each one of us has some big, major problem at an emotional level, which once it manifests will not disappear. What you need to do is to mentally recognise what is your strongest emotional problem, what it is that really disturbs your meditation.

When you have identified it, we will see how you may be able to deal with it, but first you have to identify it. A doctor first has to diagnose the disease before curing it. If something in your mind always causes lots of disturbance, you need to get to the root of it. When you are able to really identify the source of this upheaval, as far as Buddhism is concerned, there's always a solution for it. This method is more intensive than letting the mind relax and therefore you should start by applying it for a very short period of time. If it were a longer period of time, your mind would get completely uptight, angry and upset. This is because your mind is used to rampaging all over the place without any discipline. So when you give it this strict regime, when you really impose this strict discipline, it reacts strongly: it doesn't want to be caught. Nevertheless, because you only apply the method for a short time, none of you will go crazy. You can take it as an 'emergency session'!

Usually we apply more gentle methods, we bring the mind back gently in order to avoid such strong reactions. If we are sort of 'regular meditators', if we learn to be relaxed, then we don't have to apply any method, because in a true session of meditation, there isn't anything we need to do, except be aware of everything. But we haven't reached this level yet. We are all still very 'solid'. Our mind is engaging in so many thoughts and emotions that even if we know about simplicity, our mind cannot apply these instructions and we get upset. The only way then is to use other methods.

The Buddha taught 84,000 different methods; this is one of them. We need to see why we can't keep the same level of mind all the time. We need to find out what is bothering us all the time, what's causing emotions, creating chaos. In this case, our objective is to find out the root of our major problem. However, if we are always soft on ourselves, we won't make any progress. But what is fifteen minutes? We won't die in such a short time! So let's find out. Let's focus and bring our mind back forcefully. We may think it's terrible, it may give us headaches, but it will help us to see what poison, what strong energy is coming up.

Dealing with emotions

When you have identified your major problem, whatever the poison, whatever the problem is that is bothering you terribly, you should then sit there, relax, and call up this emotion in your meditation. Whether it is anger, jealousy, pride, envy, whatever, summon it here. Then introduce yourself to this 'being' which has somehow caused so much chaos in your life for so long, and investigate this feeling of yours. How big is it? Is it oblong? Round? Black? White? What colour, what shape is it?

Look at the essence of this emotion that makes you suffer so much. You always think that the emotion is genuinely happening, but if that were the case, it should have a shape, a colour, a size. If you are bothered by something, there must be something there for you to be bothered by! How can anything bother you when you find nothing? If it were a solid entity, really existing in some part of your body, you could just remove it with an operation and thus solve all your problems. However, emotions have no such characteristics.

This is the time to do a really proper investigation through meditation. Hopefully you will come to the very strong conclusion that there isn't anything to worry about, because there is nothing to be found. You then discover that you are responsible for creating emotions that do not really exist, and that you yourself transform them into solid realities.

That's why our emotional states are so difficult to handle. Somehow we are able to build this solid image out of an emotion, and it bothers us all the time. It takes away our peace and destroys whatever we're doing. If I were to tell you there is nothing to bother you, you would certainly reply, 'Oh, this Lama Yeshe is saying so, but my feelings really bother me.' This is why I'm asking you to do this investigation here, now, in your own meditation. There is no other way. When you yourself come to the conclusion that there is actually nothing there to bother you, then you should be relieved. It should comfort you to know that somehow you have been enslaved by feelings that do not really exist.

Doing this again and again is like dismantling the imagery you have built up all your life. Through meditation, you can dismantle this feeling that there is something bothering you all the time. But unless you do proper research, you won't be able to achieve it. You have to wholeheartedly involve and engage yourself in this investigation, so that you really find out for yourself. Whichever way you look, no matter how much time you invest, you find nothing at all, but if you still let your life be poisoned by this, you're really wrong, aren't you? If you can find nothing, then why should you be afraid?

For example, if you're very afraid, look at the essence of what you are afraid of. Does this fear manifest like a monster? Does it have many horns, or teeth? What is it you are really afraid of? And if you can't find anything, then think whether in childhood maybe someone frightened you. Maybe you built your own image on this and weren't able to get rid of it afterwards, although there isn't really anything to bother you now.

This type of meditation is called lhakthong in Tibetan, which means thorough investigation leading to insight.

Learning to deal with our emotions, we gradually get used to the idea of the possibility of inner transformation. In the Tibetan tradition, we say that our mind is like a wild being. We have to tame this wild being. Usually, people think that everybody else is the problem and that they themselves are the perfect ones - that way they end up never finding any peace in their minds. The right approach is to tame our own wild being and then everything else falls nicely into place. This can only be achieved through meditation.

However, things are not going to change overnight. For some, it may take ten, twenty years or more. As Buddhists, we believe that this accumulation of habits may have taken many lifetimes. Those who do not believe in previous lives can still accept the fact that it has taken them twenty, thirty or fourty years to assimilate their 'family lineage', culture, and tradition. We have so many habits, we cannot suddenly drop them altogether. That is why we should never get impatient. We should simply acknowledge that the task is difficult, but we should never give up.

Acceptance and letting go

If meditators lead lives based on selfishness, they are likely to bring exactly the same approach to their meditation and will be short-tempered, angry, uptight meditators. If their ambition is to have a completely silent mind, and people close-by make noises, they will think that all these people around them are disturbing their meditation and taking away their peace of mind! Eventually, every noise will become their enemy. When we think like that, we become very emotional, and then where is our meditation? Therefore, if we notice that we are becoming short-tempered, uptight and getting headaches, we should know that we are meditating in a wrong way. Never allow yourself to meditate like that!

Noise is a challenge. If we can make it part of our meditation, we will really make progress. If we are able to somehow incorporate the noise into our meditation, we will feel confident that we can literally meditate in the middle of the traffic. Noise can no longer bother us.

While meditating, some people get disturbed by what they see. They close their eyes in order not to see what is in front of them, but then something else will start disturbing them. They want to get rid of all sorts of things and their sight becomes their enemy. Meditation should not be an excuse to blame something or somebody for taking away our inner peace. This is a wrong way of thinking, because if we accept everything that comes our way, then nothing can bother us anymore and our inner peace is there all the time. The point is that whatever obstacle arises, if a meditator blames that for not finding inner peace, then eventually every object becomes our enemy.

Let me give you an example from my own life. When I began my long retreat in Woodstock, New York, I had a nice house next to the monastery and all the conditions were wonderful for practice, so I was very happy.

However, soon after my retreat started, the monastery decided to start a major building project right next to my house. The whole area became a building site, full of heavy machinery, so my whole house was shaking. They even cut off my electricity and water supply! I was very upset - I felt that my retreat was ruined. It gave me so much trouble I could hardly meditate.

Things got really bad and I was so upset by the noise and shaking, but then my teacher came to see me and said: 'the noise is your meditation'. This really helped me. I stopped fighting it, and began to accept it. This was a real turning point. It is very important for a practitioner to accept noise. If you don't, if noise becomes your enemy, then eventually everything will be your enemy and you will be unable to practise. During your meditation if you are bothered with noise instead of seeing it as your enemy, you should make it your friend. So this was a very important lesson for me.

However, maybe my 'noise' karma was not yet exhausted, because when I did my second retreat at Samye Ling in Scotland, I had a beautiful quiet house with a porch, and then the monastery decided to rebuild the Purelands Retreat Centre right on my doorstep. So again the whole place became a building site! In fact, the workers began to pile up their tools and dusty bags of cement right inside my porch! But it was okay for me. I began to think, 'Lama Yeshe, you must meditate for them. They are working so hard, they are building a retreat centre for others to practise the Dharma. You must practise for them.' So I encourage all of you to work with noise and disturbance and not to feel that they are obstacles. Then you can meditate anywhere and find peace no matter what.

Meditation means simple acceptance. How can we talk about being 'non-judgmental', 'non-grasping', if we have so many judgements in our mind, expecting certain feelings out of our meditation and completely rejecting some other experiences? People who adopt such an attitude are in a way like boxers going into the ring. They are thumping and punching, but they are the losers, because there is actually nobody to box! For a good meditator, all mental activities are nothing more than clouds in the sky. They come from nowhere and disappear into nowhere.

Many people come to tell me that it's an easy thing to say, but that these are 'real' things happening! 'Real' things are happening because you let yourself think it is 'really happening'! If you go on insisting that it's really there, I ask you again, how big is it, what shape, size and colour does it have? If you answer that it has none of these material characteristics, then how can you call it a 'real' thing happening? You made it real!

We build up things like, for instance, 'friends'. We think we really like a person and start thinking of all his/her good qualities. We build it up and that person gets better and better every day! But when things turn sour, we start seeing faults and the next day we notice more and more. Our belief in the reality of our feelings is what causes so much unhappiness - unnecessary unhappiness. These feelings may start as something very small but day after day we nurture them and make them grow. Whenever you meditate and you think that 'real things' are truly happening, just investigate what is there. Instead of running away, confront them and say, 'OK, I want to introduce myself to you. I want to know you better.' If you really approach it that way, you will realise that nothing is actually happening.

Physical pain

When meditating, we are often confronted with physical pain. When I was in retreat in America, I was having a lot of pain in the back and I will soon explain how you can relieve some of the pain through a proper posture. Nevertheless, most of the pain is related to the busy-ness in our minds.

We can use the lhakthong method to investigate the pain. It's simple if you really have a stable and strong will power. Marpa - the forefather of the Kagyu school of Tibetan Buddhism - taught about how you can dissolve physical pain. If you sit and experience pain, focus on the pain, look into it: how did it happen, why is it there, what colour, what shape does it have? And gradually, gradually, somehow you become part of that pain, or pain becomes part of you and you no longer feel it as painful.

Of course, this is a temporary experience and the painful feeling comes back, but being able to get rid of the pain through analysing it properly once gives you more confidence. You've done it once so you know it's definitely possible.

Once, in my monastery, my students told me: 'Lama, you are not teaching, you are only meditating!' I thought I was actually giving them the very best teaching: how to accept pain and suffering. How can we say we are learning something when we don't actually accept that we have this on-going pain and suffering every day and run away from it? Learning to meditate means learning to accept that, as long as this ego is here, we have to accept suffering. We can only be free from suffering when we fully understand the nature of true emptiness.

If you have read the life story of Milarepa, you know that he was able to overcome and get rid of pain forever. You can see this in the story of how he died. A very rich and learned Geshe who lived in the area where Milarepa was teaching, became very jealous of Milarepa's fame and achievements. He promised his secret lady friend a large turquoise if she would give a bowl of yoghurt mixed with strong poison to Milarepa. When she went to give it to him, Milarepa sent her back without taking the yoghurt and told her to bring it back later. This made her very worried that Milarepa knew about the poison, so in order to persuade her to bring it back a second time, the Geshe gave her the turquoise. When she brought the yoghurt to Milarepa he drank it and said: 'So have you been given the turquoise for what you are doing?' Milarepa knew that if she had succeeded the first time, the Geshe would not have given it to her.

When Milarepa became very ill, the Geshe couldn't believe that it was possible to bear the pain of such a strong poison, so he told Milarepa to transfer the pain to him. But when Milarepa did that the Geshe fell in complete agony, the pain and suffering was so intense that he could not bear it for even one minute.

That experience turned the Geshe into a good person. All those years he had not had any good feelings towards Milarepa. He was totally ignorant and very jealous, and he wasn't even a good Geshe, and Milarepa knew this. A Buddha can use even death for the benefit of others and Milarepa knew that if he couldn't liberate the Geshe, the only path he could go was downwards because he had accumulated so much bad karma. Milarepa wanted to liberate him. That's total forgiveness, liberating your enemy first because he has committed so many sins. So even Milarepa's death was purely motivated. It was an activity of liberation.

Afterwards the Geshe felt such deep remorse for his actions that he offered all his wealth to Milarepa's disciples and then pursued the path so diligently that he is supposed to have attained realisation.

Physical pain no longer meant anything to Milarepa, but for us, we should learn how to avoid and release unnecessary pain. The need to check and correct one's posture has just been mentioned. I will now describe this proper posture.

The Seven Point Posture

When Marpa returned to Tibet from India, he announced that he had brought back a profound teaching which was better and more effective than any teaching that had ever been brought to Tibet before. This was the Seven Point Posture.

When we meditate, we need to synchronize body and mind. The mind can benefit from teachings but the body does not understand words, it cannot learn from them. The body needs a good body posture. This is why this Seven Point Posture is taught and why we should aim to eventually sit like that.

1. The first point of the posture is sitting crossed-legged in a half or full vajra posture. This means sitting like the Buddha.

When I was very slim, I could sit in full vajra posture for many hours. Recently, I went into retreat and tried to sit in this full vajra posture. I sat for half an hour and couldn't undo it! It hurt so much! I then thought that this posture was no longer going to work for me any more. Before, it was all right, but now.... so much pain! Age must have something to do with it. Therefore if you cannot sit like that, it's fine, just do what you can.

When we are learning to meditate, we shouldn't worry too much about physical problems, because the calmer our mind is, the less pain we will experience. If our mind is uptight and we have mental difficulties, no matter how we sit, we will experience physical pain.

When our mind is calm, hours can go by without our noticing our body. Let's see who is the boss, the mind or the body? Physical recovery, good health, everything starts with having a calm, peaceful and positive state of mind. It is the mind that gives the signals and triggers physical reactions. Everything comes from the mind; everything starts there. We should remember that our mind is the boss. We should try not to run away from the pain but remain seated and calm.

When I complained to one of the great Lamas, Kalu Rinpoche, about the pain I was experiencing when I was in retreat in America, he told me that pain is part of the meditation. But I don't think this would be very popular with a European audience, and I think we can make some concessions. We don't really need to go through so much pain if it can be released.

Especially in the beginning, when we experience physical pain, we shouldn't try to sit through it. It is a question of flexibility and, of course, nobody likes to torture themselves if they can help it. If we need to extend our legs, we can do so, but gently, so as not to completely disturb our meditation. We can sometimes easily avoid pain through improving or changing our posture. During the meditation, we can try to sit in different postures, to use different visualisations and different methods. If nothing really helps, if the pain is still there, maybe this is only because we haven't been working hard enough to find a solution. People should experiment.

For people who experience a lot of pain in the knees when they sit cross-legged on the floor, there is maybe nothing much they can do except to sit on a chair. I can understand it: Westerners are not used to sitting on the floor, they were brought up to sit on chairs. If you can meditate on a chair and straighten up the upper part of your body, it is also very good, and gradually, when you become very calm mentally, you can gather the courage to sit cross-legged and maybe you will find one day that there is no more pain.

If you experience pain in the back and lower hips, it means that your body posture is not right. You can actually improve your body posture and lessen the physical pain. When the sitting posture is not right, the bones of your backbone touch and rub each other. Pulling up the head pulls your whole body upwards. When you straighten up the backbone likewise, it helps you to feel more comfortable.

2. The second point of the posture is to put our hands one on top of the other: the right hand on the palm of the left hand, palms upward, thumbs touching each other, approximately four fingers below our navel. We don't have to measure precisely, roughly there is good enough.

3. It is also said that we should straighten our arms. That makes many people think they have very long arms! There are a few ways to 'shorten' our arms, for instance by sitting on a higher cushion. Our previous retreat master at Samye Ling used to go around and twist the arms of the students to get them straight. Sometimes it is easier to have someone else to help us rather than trying to do it ourselves. The shoulders should also be extended like an eagle's wings. When we straighten our arms, our shoulder blades naturally touch at the back and we are like an eagle spreading its wings. You may think that this teaching is pure physical torture, but this is only because your body is used to unwholesome habits. Taking this posture is actually the first time you are giving your body a useful habit!

4. The fourth point is bending the neck like a hook. We pull up the head and the chin is slightly dropped. In Tibet, some yogis are rather 'fanatic'. They twist their long hair up in a knot and attach it to a hook fixed in the ceiling: no chance of sleeping! Others have a stick with a moon-shaped structure at the top to hold their chin, and they tie it up to their body like a bandage so that they can't fall. But I'm not recommending you to try this, because if you tie yourself up and fall down, you won't be able to get up again! Meditaters have tried many things. Sometimes, when they don't want to fall asleep, they put a dorje in front of them and if they fall asleep, their forehead hits the dorje. The pain guarantees they will stay awake for many hours!

5. The fifth point is that our backbone should be straight like an arrow. This is actually very good for the body. If our body is very straight, our backbone will be much stronger in the long run.

6. The sixth point is that our two eyes should focus at a point roughly four fingers from our nose. We are not looking at our nose but gazing into space about four fingers below. And, according to these Mahamudra instructions, the eyes should be fixed, not blinking. Nevertheless, our gaze should be relaxed, without tension. We are looking into space and space is wide, deep and vast.

7. The seventh point is the mouth. The lips should be neither open nor closed, just gently set in the natural way. At the same time, the tongue should touch the upper palate, which stops the production of too much saliva. In addition, in order to be free from three faults, a meditator should sit very comfortably, very lightly and very loosely. This is the proper Seven Point Posture.

In the beginning, it may seem unnecessarily uncomfortable but with some regular practice, it will become easier and even very comfortable. For example, in the retreat, everybody thought that it was impossible in the beginning, but later they all adapted to the posture.

Knowing the benefits of the posture will also definitely help you. European minds are very curious and always need to have a reason why they should do something. If there is no reason, why should one bother to keep this difficult posture? I will therefore explain what benefits come from this proper posture and what harm may result from not sitting properly.

The benefits of right posture

According to the Mahamudra teachings, if we do not have a proper body posture, no matter how much effort we make, we will have a hard time improving our meditation.

There are 72,000 nadis (energy channels) and six chakras (wheels of energy) in the subtle body. They are responsible for the energy of the body and linked with the mental activity. The energy currents can be compared to a horse and the thoughts to the rider of the horse. If our physical body is straight, the nadi or energy channels are also straight so that the prana (energy) flows properly and our mental activity comes under our control. On the contrary, if our body is bent, body and mind get imbalanced and instead of finding inner peace, we will get more disturbed and confused. Therefore we have a better chance of achieving inner peace and improving our meditation when sitting with a proper body posture.

The benefits of adopting this Seven Point Posture are as follows:

Our body has two types of energy: one is going upward and the other downward. The energy moving downward is usually lost and therefore wasted. When we sit cross-legged, it stops us losing that downward energy and helps us bring it into the 'uma', the central channel.

Apart from the 72,000 nadis, we have three main channels in the subtle body. The 'uma' is the central channel and the two other channels run parallel to it on each side. The prana or energies are connected with the 'mind poisons' or disturbing emotions and thoughts. The purpose of all our practice is to get rid of these negative emotions, or rather transform them, and a proper body posture can support that process. We can imagine that the 'uma' is like a huge furnace that burns everything, cutting the mind poisons straight at their very root. When we are able to bring the downward flowing life energy into the central channel, that energy is connected to the poison of jealousy and we will gradually be able to subdue jealousy.

When we put our hands on top of one another, it helps bring what we call the 'water-wind energy' into the central channel. That 'water-wind energy' is connected to anger. When we bring this water energy into the central channel, we are able to reduce and pacify anger.

Straightening up the arms and shoulders will help us bring the 'earth-wind energy' into the central channel. That energy seems to be related to ignorance and bringing it into the central channel enables us to overcome our ignorance.

Shaping the neck and throat like a hook helps us bring the 'fire-wind energy' connected to the poison of desire or attachment, into the central channel, which will help us reduce it.

Focusing our eyes and putting the tip of our tongue against our palate will help us bring the 'wind energy' into the central channel. We will then be able to reduce or overcome pride, which is related to that energy.

We can consider the channels as highways through which the energy-winds travel. If we take the time to learn these methods properly, we will find they bring us great benefit.

Just being able to take a proper physical posture will help us overcome these five poisons. That is a great achievement. If we can keep it, we should gradually train to perfect it. If we cannot, we shouldn't however worry too much about it, but just do the best we can.

As I have already explained, during our meditation, we can investigate and find out what mind poison most strongly affects us and thus identify our biggest problem. We are all subject to the various mind poisons, but they do not manifest in the same way for everybody. Each person is more under the influence of one or several specific mind poisons whereas the other poisons are less manifest. When we have identified our main emotional problem, we should put more emphasis on the aspects of the correct posture linked to it. This is one way of working on the strongest emotional problem that is the biggest obstacle to our development.

Obstacles due to incorrect posture

If we do not adopt the Seven Point Posture we may encounter obstacles in our meditation. If our body is not straight, then the prana, the mind and the body do not synchronize and many thoughts are thus generated. It is therefore more difficult to 'catch' this elusive mind without having the right sitting posture.

According to the traditional commentaries, if we are leaning towards the right side when we sit, we may experience a feeling of clarity in the beginning but it will gradually turn into anger. If our body is leaning to the left, in the beginning we will feel blissful and comfortable, but after a while, the bliss will gradually turn into desire. If our body leans towards the front - and this happens very often if we feel sleepy! - in the beginning we will get the impression that we have realized something: we have an experience of no thought and emptiness, but it will turn into ignorance. According to Buddhism, sleep is ignorance! If our body is bending backwards, in the beginning there is a sort of feeling of emptiness that will gradually turn into pride.

According to the Mahamudra texts, if we are able to adopt the Seven Point Posture properly, it will stop the arising of these faults and bring the benefit of overcoming all the poisons. This is why posture is an important part of the practice. Otherwise, it would seem an impossible job. Now we know what to do if we want to get rid of the five mind-poisons: adopt the Seven Point Posture. And if we want to increase the five poisons, we also know what to do!

So I think these are good reasons to sit in front of a mirror and check how you sit. Every home has mirrors and my recommendation is that you should sit in front of a mirror for a while. If you see that you are leaning this way or that way, you can change your posture by adjusting the cushion. You don't have to change your body, the cushion can make it happen. It is as easy and as simple as that. So don't be afraid.

Despite all I have just said, you should not worry too much about this body posture. If you start worrying, maybe you will be so afraid of doing something wrong that you will end up doing no meditation at all. The whole idea of these instructions is not to frighten you but to help you improve your meditation.

One should meditate with no hope and no fear. People often think that if they have no hope or expectations, there is no point in doing anything. However, as soon as we have hope, fear automatically comes. If we want to get rid of the fear, we have to get rid of the hope as well. Be it in our professional or family life, whatever we do, the minute we think we need something or we want something, fear is there. If there is no hope, there is no fear. In fact, it is the Buddha nature itself that does the whole job, therefore we don't have to hope for anything. It just happens.

Just to repeat, I can definitely understand those who cannot sit cross-legged or on the floor. They can sit on a chair and apply the proper body posture to the upper part of the body and it is then very similar to sitting on the floor. You should allow your body enough time to adapt to the posture. It may take a long time and some people might be too old to change their body in this lifetime because it no longer has the flexibility of youth. There is no point in forcing it, which would only result in damaging your body. If this is your case, you shouldn't worry too much about achieving the proper posture in this life. Most important is to keep the spine straight, which you can do simply by sitting on a chair. If you practice meditation regularly, you will gradually 'plant the right seeds' and you may be equipped with a body capable of taking the proper sitting posture in your next life.

Integrating the Dharma in one's daily life

I think you all know that trying to practise Dharma by yourself in the city is very difficult. Unless you have strong will-power and discipline, you'll find so many excuses why you can't practice Dharma. This is why Dharma centres in the city are very meaningful and very useful. Such centres help people living in the city to integrate the Dharma into their life. Indeed, even if they can find hundreds of excuses not to practise every day, if they can just find the time to come to the centre once or twice a week, it is still very beneficial. As you know, to practise Dharma is the way one can find inner peace.

Dharma centres welcome you and provide you with a structure, with teachers, with a place to learn and practice meditation in a beautiful shrine room, and with on-going activities, such as different sadhanas every evening. This is all very positive. As far as integrating our practice into daily life is concerned, I think Dharma centres are the only places that can re-energize you. It will give you inspiration to see other people practise or being confronted with the same problems as the ones you face yourself.

Some people refuse to take part in a group to learn meditation. They think they can learn meditation alone at home, but that is very difficult. People who try to meditate at home may have a family with children who make noise and disturb their meditation. If they've been busy working all day, when they sit and meditate, their mind will be looking for any excuse to make them get up. They will suddenly remember that they should clean this room, fix the house, prepare their shopping list or that they forgot something very important. They end up doing all the things they 'forgot' to do and it proves more or less impossible to start any meditation.

A beginner will also make the slightest mental or physical pain an excuse to give up, whereas in a group, people have enough ego to remain sitting even if they're going through a lot of physical pain. They can't see anybody else standing up and walking out, so their ego kindly keeps them seated with the others. If, as a beginner, you can sit there for half an hour and if the next day you find it impossible to sit for even fifteen minutes at home, then you should really question why. Therefore, learning in a group is very useful when beginning to meditate.

However, if you want to progress, a regular daily practice is necessary and therefore, you should have a place where you can meditate at home. For your own benefit, you should ideally have a small room, a small shrine room if possible, a cushion, and nothing else, no pen, no paper. Then you should really be disciplined and tell yourself that whatever comes in your mind, you're not going follow it. If you don't have such a structure and discipline, you will never manage to do any practice.

Many people are strongly inspired to practise after having attended a meditation course, but their enthusiasm is often like a big fire that burns very strong and bright but dies out very quickly. We need to keep the fire burning somehow. For example, every morning when we wake up we can remind ourselves how fortunate we are to be alive, how precious and fragile life is and how important it is to use every moment in a meaningful way. If we start our day by wondering why we have to get up and by feeling miserable, everything goes wrong from the start. Meditation should help us transform our bad habits into positive ones. It should free us from the control of negative thought patterns and help us become positive and useful human beings who appreciate what they have. We cannot afford to be negative. Keeping the inspiration alive means that we will feel good about ourselves all the time.

As far as a proper sitting meditation schedule is concerned, we should know that there are two types of energy. One is called the rising or increasing energy and the second the decreasing energy. Normally, there is increasing energy in the morning and decreasing energy in the afternoon. In the morning, the sun comes up, birds and people wake up, it brings life back. In the afternoon, the sun gradually goes down, the birds disappear, even the flowers close up their petals. No matter how much effort we invest, we are losing energy and things are much more difficult to achieve. There is much less benefit meditating in the afternoon.

So the idea is that many of us need to change our habits. Maybe there is no harm in waking up a little earlier. If we wake up thirty minutes earlier to meditate, why not go to bed thirty minutes earlier if we think we really need ten hours sleep? We monks believe that five hours of good sleep is all we need. Everything is a question of habits. The earlier we get up in the morning, the more we will appreciate this really wonderful world out there. If we sleep late, we get lots of headaches and when we hurry to our office, we don't even notice the weather and all the nice things in the world that can only be seen in the morning.

The whole idea is to get up early. When the alarm rings, don't think, 'Wait a minute, wait a minute!' No excuse. That doesn't work. When it rings, jump out! No thinking. Just jumping out is the solution. To start procrastinating is a disaster. I tried this you know. 'Oh, just one more minute...' Then I woke up two hours later. No good! Gradually, we won't even need to set the alarm, we will get so used to it that we will just naturally wake up at the right time. We should have a steady commitment. If we decide to give ourselves thirty minutes in the morning and thirty minutes in the evening, we should never compromise. If we have a headache, still we should practice. If we feel miserable, still we should practice. If we are over-excited, still we should practice. This way steadiness will develop. When we are practising steadily, we will see the change and then devotion, faith and belief will grow.

Meditation means skilfully working on ourselves from the minute we get up till the minute we go to sleep, always remaining mindful, not getting emotionally involved with everybody and everything, so that we can somehow maintain our inner calm. If we can maintain this calm, it will be easy to sit and meditate daily for twenty minutes. But if we get angry and upset during the whole day, it will only get worse in the meditation. Instead of sitting for twenty minutes, we will go away after only five seconds, because we won't be able to deal with our inner chaos. Therefore, to really benefit from the practice, this awareness should be brought into every moment of our life. When we find this peace, ease and comfort, then we make progress.

Buddha's teachings are for all sentient beings. To be a good person, one does not have to become a monk or a nun or to live in a monastery. Family life offers us more challenges than any other situation. It is just a question of slowly, patiently and skilfully changing our habits through meditation. We should gather the courage to sit down, calm down, reflect, confront our weaknesses and push back our limits a little further all the time. We may then discover that many problems we consider a big deal may not really be such a big deal, they somehow dissolve of their own accord.

Everybody has to earn a living, and you may all be working in different environments. If you are an angry, bossy person, you will bring these reactions with you to your workplace, and give the people around you much unnecessary suffering. Meditation will bring you more understanding of the situation. You will see that you have to get along with your colleagues and subordinates who are earning their living just as you are, and not make them miserable. Of course, some of them are not always capable of doing everything right, but you have to accept this. Why should you make things worse by reminding them how bad they are, especially in public? There is no kindness in blaming others, thinking how much better and quicker you are at doing everything. Nobody is perfect. One should have more sympathy, be kinder, more understanding and remember that, by reacting in a harsh way, one might well plant the seeds of being reborn in the same situation as the person one criticises.

At home, if our partner, children or friends are not interested in the spiritual path, in meditation or in Buddhism, if they don't agree with what we are trying to do, we shouldn't upset them. We can plead that if we are able to get these ten or twenty minutes of meditation, we may become a much nicer person and that they will benefit from it. We should always try to solve problems by discussing them, but if the discussion doesn't work, then it's not necessary to tell them what we are doing. Instead we should use skilful means! One can always find thirty minutes somewhere, so why argue? All we need to do is to find some quiet place, and then clean it up nicely, tidy it up, make it very nice and comfortable. The best would be to have it quite bare, without too much decoration. Then we can disappear in there for a while. We shouldn't take any pen, pencil or paper with us. Even very important things can wait, we shouldn't write them down or we will lose our meditation. If we decide to give ourselves thirty minutes, then unless our house is burning down, we should stay there, otherwise we will always find so many excuses. Every time, we will remember something to do instead. That should not happen.

If we have to make it secret, then find a secret place. If our family and friends allow us to practise openly, why not make it available for them too? I saw many young children play around next to their parents and, in this peaceful environment, gradually become quieter, learn meditation and become good meditators - which is very good.

If we are learning to meditate or we are interested in different religions, we should not talk about it to everybody, because some people are quite negative. At work we should never advertise our practice of meditation. Sometimes, when people learn about meditation, they get so inspired that they want to tell everybody and convince others to do the same. I think there is no need to talk about it. Why should we have to tell everybody? If we look at our motivation, we might well discover that it is just ego wishing others to see how good, how special we are. But it might have the opposite result. Others may not see what we do as admirable and great, but rather think we are strange, engaging in a wrong activity, and then we may get upset or feel ashamed about what other people say about us. But who told them in the first place? If we hadn't told them, they wouldn't have known anything. Some people may argue that they have to be 'honest' and 'true', but honest to whom? By keeping silent, we are not cheating or harming anybody; instead we avoid creating problems. Talking can bring problems. If people show interest, then it is our duty to talk, but there is no need to try to influence others or make them believe what we believe.

Anyway, we won't need to say anything to those closest to us, because if they see us becoming better human beings than we were before, they will come to ask what we are doing and maybe they will wish to try themselves. The idea is to be very skilful and not to talk unless somebody asks and appreciates what we are doing.

When we meditate in the morning, we calm our mind and before starting our daily activities, we remember the things we want to change and our wish to use our four activities of walking, sitting, eating and sleeping, as a practice. We anticipate the challenges that we might encounter and most of all we rekindle our intention to develop awareness throughout the day.

Maintaining clarity and a positive attitude is very important. We must always keep to the right view. Having the right view means that, if you get up in the morning feeling terrible, you don't let this feeling affect your whole day by giving your family and colleagues a hard time. Instead you just shake your head and think how lucky, how very fortunate you are not to be dead! Being able to look at situations in this way is essential, because how we see things in the morning affects our whole day. You need to remember to keep this positive state of mind and have a clear direction. Tell yourself, 'I'm a decent human being. If I can't change the world for the better, at least I will never contribute to the world getting worse.'

When you are confronted with a challenge, remember it is something you want to deal with. As soon as you remember this, it is as if your finger was on a switchboard. You can switch off the negative emotion because, at the start, an emotion is very weak. People sometimes tell me that they cannot apply this method. This is because they don't remember to switch off at the right time. If they let the emotion grow, it becomes much stronger and more difficult to control. If you are caught unaware, when somebody shouts at you or says something unpleasant, you will react with anger. Many people get upset or angry so quickly. They react like lightning and in the end they can only feel sorry for themselves and for the pain they have caused around them.

That is why this whole practice is based on bringing inner peace. It means that we should first find inner peace. When we become a peaceful human being, our whole family will benefit. And somehow, if we are not there to argue with them, they will also find inner peace. If our whole family finds inner peace, our whole neighbourhood will benefit. This is how, I think, we can make our world better. Otherwise we tell everybody what they have to do, while we ourselves remain very angry human beings. We do not do anything to change on our side, but we tell other people what they have to do. That doesn't work and doesn't change anything.

Indeed, if you're angry, if you have no clarity, you will be causing lots of chaos and be an active participant in the deterioration of this world. Whereas if you are more stable and you're able to have your own direction, you don't create any chaos and at the same time, by helping others to share the same approach, you're actually contributing to changing the world for the better. It's like a transmission.

If in your home everybody feels good, that's very nice. But if one person feels miserable and it affects you so you also get sad and unhappy because of what is happening in the family, this won't do you any good, and it will prevent you from helping others. A cloudy sky can cover the sun. In the same way, our positive mind gets clouded by negative thoughts and emotions. Unless you're very, very strong, the energies produced by the people around you, your friends, your partner, the members of your family, can also affect your life. Therefore, when pursuing a spiritual path, if you feel strong and well, you should guide your friends and relatives in the right direction, show them the right view, so that they can benefit from your achievements. But you need to always remember that you should never give in to their negativities. To have a direction, to have this sense of purpose, means you have to take the strong decision never to submit to other people's negativities. It doesn't matter whether they are your family or friends. If you join their club, if you suffer and feel as negative as they do, that won't do any good either to you or to them. You need to really come out of this, and then do everything you can to help them, to pull them out, through meditation and your good example, showing them how it can be done.

Nowadays, so many so-called intelligent, successful people lead a life of arrogance, selfishness and insatiable greed. It actually causes a lot of harm to other people as well as to themselves because they lose all their friends and end up feeling miserable and lonely.

To start meditating indicates a wish to improve one's situation. If you are one of these successful people who have lots of egoistic ideas and care about nobody but yourself, you should, through practising, lower the temperature and bring yourself to a middle path. On the other hand, there are also many people who have a very low self-esteem because of all the successive failures they have gone through. I have noticed that in the West, many people lack self-confidence and have quite a bad image of themselves. They have been put down by what others have said about their lack of intelligence or education. Parents can be the worst offenders! Parents always expect their children to be the best and make them feel useless if they are not. They tell them that they are not good enough or that their studies or their jobs are not good enough. When you hear this all the time, you start feeling that it may be true.

It is also due to modern civilisation. People make judgements so easily. Someone who doesn't succeed a few times in their life is immediately considered a failure. People in this situation should remember what the Buddha taught about every being's potential. We are all equal, and we all have the potential to become a Buddha. We should not be judgmental towards our failures and end up torturing ourselves. Everybody experiences failure at least once in his or her life. We have this potential to become what we want to be. We should never let somebody else tell us who we are or decide who we should be. We should stop listening to people putting us down and start being self-confident!

You see, our attitude has to be balanced, without extremes, without either arrogance or low self-esteem. We should always remember the Buddha's teachings on Buddha nature. This Buddha nature is the same for everybody. We should learn to recognise and respect our potential, but also understand that there is no space for pride and feelings of superiority, because we all have an equal potential.

Mahamudra in daily life means sharpening our awareness. When we are walking, we are aware that we are walking. When we are talking, we know that we are talking. When we are driving, we remember we are in our car driving and we can recite vajra mantras. Sometimes, I walk in the busy streets and I get headaches: so many people running around like ants, without goal or aim, looking lost as if they were crazy.

When this happens, I think the best way is to remember to recite a mantra. It gives you stability - what we call one-pointedness. If you can just mentally recite a mantra, then your mind and body are not dissociated and walking becomes very meaningful. It's called vajra recitation. You don't have to shout the mantra. People would think you're crazy. You can recite the mantra in your mind. What you can do is, when you're going to your job, or to the office, instead of aimlessly watching what people are doing, or paying attention to how they behave, try to be more 'centered' within yourself. You can recite 'Om Mani Peme Hung', it's a very good mantra because it's the essence of all the Buddhas' loving and kindness. You can remember that you're reciting this mantra because you want to develop loving kindness.

You then go to your job as a wholesome being. And once you're in the workplace, you can have this mantra written somewhere, and whenever you get a glimpse of it, it will remind you to recite it mentally. This will reduce your need to talk meaningless talk.

Mentally reciting a mantra is very powerful. You can recite a mantra mentally anywhere and it reminds you to be aware of everything. When you remember to recite a mantra, when you are aware, you don't make mistakes, you remain calm in any situation. Even in the workplace, if somebody upsets you, you will not become angry because you're very focused, very 'together'. You remember that jumping at the first provocation is not the right way.

It also helps you to stop hearing things you don't want to hear. You may decide to reduce needless communication with others, but if your ears still listen to everything that's going on around you, you may hear someone say very bad things about you and then you'll get really upset. You'll start thinking, 'How can he/she say such things about me!' and you'll be ready to fight back. Therefore, if you're going to reduce talking, also stop listening. It's the only way, and it's very simple. What's the point of listening to people gossiping? They can say anything they wish, what does it matter?

If you're a really good practitioner, you will understand that 'all sounds are perfect, all sounds are pure and have no solidity' When you have a really wonderful experience taking place on that day, then people may call you the worst names, but for you it's just beautiful sounds. In the Vajrayana approach, all sounds are empty, and we are the ones who stick labels on them, identifying them as bad, good, right, wrong, etc... We make all this up. If other people are saying something while you're reciting mantras, then it doesn't matter what they're saying, in your mind they are simply reciting mantras too. Their words are just sounds and the essence of sound is pure. The meaning of the words doesn't really matter to you anymore. This is how a good practitioner uses his or her skill to disassociate themselves from getting involved and entangled with what happens all around.

When you recite mantras, you may sometimes feel sorry for these people who don't actually know what they're talking about. Of course, you don't have to be arrogant and tell them, 'Oh, I'm so sorry for you!' This would make them very angry and your aim is certainly not to create more problems! You should always use wisdom, which means you don't have to express everything you think. People who express whatever's going though their mind have lost clarity and have no control over their speech. If you really feel very sorry for someone who's using their speech in a wrong way, the best would be to include this person in your prayers and practice. That is much more meaningful.

In a way, the Vajrayana practice is one of the best types of practice for the Western mind because, in spite of all the complaints you have about Tibetan Buddhism being complicated and crazy, your minds are no less complicated than our crazy teachings! If I'm giving you simple meditation techniques, your minds get bored and you complain. If I give you visualizations, you think it's too much. However, if you're honest with yourself, you have visualizations or daydreaming going on in your heads twenty four hours a day! What's the difference? Actually, these 'old' methods of visualizations, chanting, reciting mantras and meditation are using this ability of our mind to daydream in a wise and positive way, in order to really help us incorporate everything we do as part of our Dharma practice.

When you're eating or drinking, you visualize your physical form not just as your ordinary form, but as a deity. In the Vajrayana, this physical form is very precious and very important. If you have been practising Green Tara, White Tara, Guru Rinpoche, or any other, you can transform yourself into this deity, and then even eating and drinking become a practice because you view it as an offering to the deity. When you are walking or sitting, it's as if you are circumambulating the mandala of the universe, so that even sitting and walking become a practice. Whatever you say, your speech becomes the sound of mantras. Even sleep becomes meaningful.

How you go to sleep is most important. If you go to sleep feeling very nervous, very negative, you might have nightmares, bad dreams or less sleep. If you sleep with ignorance or bad thoughts, you are brewing bad karma even during your sleep. But if you're able to go to sleep with a very positive, stable and clear mind, not letting mundane thoughts and emotions take over, then even sleep becomes a practice.

I think that's why we say that Buddhism, and Vajrayana in particular, is good for everybody, because it means your eating, walking, sitting, talking and sleeping all become part of meditation. You can actually incorporate everything into your practice and you no longer have to worry so much about how many hours you actually spend on formal practice and sitting meditation. Your whole life has become your practice.

These are also very effective methods to sharpen our awareness. Developing and maintaining awareness is very important. For beginners, it means in this context keeping in mind, constantly remembering: 'I am offering, I am reciting, I am praying, I am sleeping in clear light.' All this sharpens your awareness and re-educates your mind. This new attitude takes the place of your old habitual patterns. This is the only thing you have to learn: to re-educate yourself and make some effort. I think it is exactly like a clean table: to keep it clean, you have to polish it all the time. Dust keeps on falling. Worldly people have bad habits, which keep coming without them having to make any effort. Trying to make it better is so difficult! Struggling, not remembering, not having enough courage, not having enough wisdom, not having enough time - so dust keeps on falling. We just need to remember: Buddha is talking about this pure mind, so we need to dust our mind every morning, every afternoon, every evening, day and night - just dusting with awareness.

The benefits of meditation

Buddha gave 84,000 different types of teachings. This is because people have different abilities and not everybody can follow the same path. If you are the type of person who likes to study and pursue different types of knowledge, then meditation might be hard for you, so you can study Buddhist philosophy and use your energy that way.

Our Kagyu lineage is called the 'practice lineage'. We put great emphasis on meditation, diligence, belief, trust and faith, because if you have no belief, it will be difficult to meditate. But if you have belief or trust, and diligence, then this practice lineage is good for you and will bring you speedy results. Through meditation you will experience within yourself everything that you may have learned from texts.

I believe that for ordinary people who have a family, meditation is the right path because, even if you only meditate for thirty minutes or one hour every day, it can enrich your life and your ability to function more effectively in this very stressful world.

Sometimes it is very useful to accept that whatever we are, whatever we go through now, is the result of our previous actions. But for the future, everything is in our own hands. We plant the seeds of our future in this life, in this present moment. We can really change our future, definitely! Sometimes, because they misunderstand the nature of karma, people think that Buddhists are determinists or fatalists. They think karma is very solid, very real. However karma, whether positive or negative, is not really fixed. I always give the example of the body and its shadow. As long as the body is solid, it has a shadow. When we realize the empty nature of everything, karma dissolves; it no longer exists. Knowing this is a source of happiness, because whatever bad karma we may have accumulated, it can be changed. Therefore we shouldn't get depressed, feeling that we are sinners without any way out. It doesn't have to be that way. Of course we have made many mistakes, but as long as we can learn from our mistakes, we really have a great potential.

Karma is no excuse for feeling hopeless and for making the same mistakes over and over again. If we improve, it will definitely have a snowball effect on our environment. Buddhism is very practical. If we become wiser, calmer, more stable, our relatives and friends will come to us to take advice. They will listen to us because our judgement is impartial, not based on our own ego and interest. In Tibet, we say that if a man wants to win the respect and esteem of his family, he cannot achieve this by selfish means. His first job will be to make his wife and children happy.

A short meditation course is not going to change your life completely, but if you can start properly and remember the key points of my instructions, then gradually, you will learn how to help yourself when you run into difficulties. If you apply these teachings, they will be of tremendous benefit to you. If you learn to meditate regularly, you will find out how to make your body and mind calm, how to accept yourself and also how to take responsibility for your own actions.

What you really need to remember is how to tame your body, speech and mind. Sometimes, we call it 'perfecting' body, speech and mind. You should know what to do with your physical actions and with your speech. As to the mind, always remember to maintain a positive attitude. If you can just remember to remain a positive human being, it will be much, much easier to tame your body and speech and there will be less chaos around you. If you try to see through a glass filled with muddy water, you won't be able to see anything through it. If you let the dirt settle, the water becomes clear, and you will see through it easily. In the same way, if your mind is always agitated and confused, you will never be able to do anything effective with your body and speech, they are just lost at an emotional level. Through meditation your mind becomes calm and clear, and you will then be able to deal with your life properly.

We should always remember that our true nature is perfect and that whatever we are going through is just a temporary habit. We need to remember that there is this light at the end of the tunnel, so that no matter how difficult what we're going through is, we know there is an end to it. We need to remember our Buddha nature, the perfect essence of our life. If we can do that, then remembering not to misuse our body and our speech becomes easy. However, trying to change this mind will take some time. It's 'inside work' and can only happen through regular practice of meditation.

Those of you who can meditate for at least thirty minutes should definitely do so. However if you find it difficult as beginners, then you should meditate at least fifteen minutes in the morning and fifteen minutes more after your job, or whenever is suitable for you. You should then examine whether you have been successful and whether you have been able to transform all your activities into practice. In this way, you will make progress. You need to keep on making this effort again and again. It is not going to be easy but the benefit will outweigh all the time and effort you put into it. You will gradually find that you are becoming a better human being and that you can deal better with situations.

Meditation is a most necessary part of our lives. If you have more or less done and achieved everything, and yet feel you're not really wholesome or fulfilled, then I think it may be the time for you to meditate and find real fulfilment through this inner understanding. I have personally seen with my own eyes the difference between practitioners and non-practitioners. When practitioners are getting old, they never feel lonely. They're prepared for death. They know this is what's going to happen. When death comes, it is an opportunity. Why should they be afraid to die? Their physical form is not functioning any longer, but their mind is sharper than ever.

When we started the traditional three-year retreats, Samye Ling didn't have a good public image. European doctors wondered what we were doing, locking people up. There was a lot of distrust on their side. During the retreat, one young guy who was helping to build Samye Ling got sick. Doctors diagnosed cancer and gave him only two more months to live. He had been in Samye Ling for many years, but he had never bothered to practise, he was just there to work. He then came to me and said, 'Look, Lama Yeshe, I have wasted all my time. When I was well, I thought I could work and practice later on. Now I'm supposed to have only a couple of months left to live, please could you help me?' He joined the retreat and I taught him how to practise. The other retreatants would also take turns looking after him. His faith and practice grew very strong and he was very happy and positive. When he was about to die, I thought he'd better go to the hospital and called a doctor. The doctor discussed it with him and came to the conclusion that he was very happy and serene, and that there was no need for him to go to the hospital. He died peacefully a couple of days later. His family were non-believers, but they all came to thank us for what we had been able to do.

A brain tumour was also diagnosed in another of our retreatants. Once again, we helped by taking care of him in the retreat. He practised and meditated and he became so positive, so happy, that the doctor had to admit, 'Your patients don't need us, we need them. Each time they come into the hospital, they change the whole atmosphere because they don't come here moaning, suffering and frightened. They are not afraid to die, their state of mind is pure and positive. They are full of joy and ready to go.'

As far as I can see through such experiences, actual proper practice does bring benefits. I tell you this because sometimes people try hard and do not notice any change. But even if the results are not immediately visible, the changes happen. It is like planting good seeds. You are weeding and ploughing the field, preparing for the good crop. It can take time, but it will definitely come. So I do hope you will not consider meditation practice as an unnecessary part of your life.

As you can see, there is a very good reason to think that you'd better find thirty minutes to meditate rather than saying, 'I'm so busy, I can't find the time.' When you die, you have to go alone - your husband or wife, your children and friends, your home and all your business won't come with you. They can't protect you. No matter how much they like you or how much you like them, separation comes. You will have to go by yourself. You came by yourself and you will go by yourself. That is the time you need to be well prepared. Meditating and practising is like accumulating true wealth that can never be taken away, even by death itself.

Practice will definitely help us at the moment of death. Many people may not believe in a life after death, but if our mind is just like this body, which disintegrates after death, or like a candle that can just be blown out, why worry about anything? However, if mind were like a candle, then when the body gets old, the mind should also get old. When the body is no longer functioning, the mind should also stop functioning. Nevertheless, if you witness people dying, you will see that they are either serene or very frightened. People who are in a positive frame of mind have the wonderful experience of seeing Christ or angels or Buddhas. People who are in a negative frame of mind are completely frightened and undergo very fearful experiences. At the very moment the body falls apart, the mind gets stronger. If you are the sort of person who doesn't believe in after-life experience, then you should really watch people dying.

In Buddhism, we are told to look forward to death. Death gives us all the possibilities. For a yogi, death is an opportunity, because what happens in your next life is in your hands, and you have the opportunity of liberation. If we have been practising, we recognize without doubt what happens at the time of death, such as the dissolution of the elements. We can prepare for death with practice and meditation, and we will then be able to die peacefully in a very positive frame of mind. I tell you this because there is no human being in this whole world who will not have to die. One day it will happen to all of us. Therefore, meditating and learning how to calm our mind in order to gain inner wisdom is absolutely essential.

Questions & Answers

Q: How should one deal with the experiences that arise during meditation?

A: According to the Buddhist teachings, the mind is like a spring field in which all kinds of plants can grow. When you are learning to meditate, many experiences will 'grow' in your mind. You have to know they are neither bad nor good. Learn to just leave them alone.

Q: Does this mean not to be afraid and not to get attached to them?

A: Yes, that's the whole purpose of meditation. We get afraid because of ego. We get attached because of ego. So we have to overcome this.

Q: Lama Yeshe, did you have to make friends with your inner obstacles?

A: Oh, definitely! Because it's your mind that says who is your enemy and who is your friend. In my opinion, many European people first need to make friends with themselves. You can only make friends with others when you're at peace with yourself. Many of you don't have much liking for yourselves. You always find something to blame.

If you think about it, this is very strange. You're serving your ego so diligently twenty-four hours a day: you don't want to be cold, you don't want to be hungry, you don't want to be unhappy.... And on the other hand, you keep on saying, 'I don't like myself, I hate myself.' If you don't like yourself, why do you constantly pamper yourself? Because you care so much for yourself, you can't tolerate anybody saying bad things to you, you can't bear to feel cold or hungry. If you care so much for yourself, then why do you say you hate yourself?

You are suffering from a kind of inside wound. What you need to do is to make it better first. Once this wound is healed, only then will you know how to take care of others. It's all a matter of attitude.

Q: I have the feeling that some things in our lives are meant to be, so they come to us effortlessly. Other things we are ambitious to achieve, but how do we do that without causing harm?

A: As you know, if you do everything right, the proper fruition comes. Suppose, say, you want to have a very good crop in a field. You don't just hope for it but you prepare the field very carefully. You plough the field, you get rid of the stones and weeds, you get pure seeds, you plant them and you know there's going to be a good crop. But if you don't do all this and still hope a good crop will come out, this is wishful thinking! Nothing will come, and if something does grow, it will be all weeds. Good preparation with wisdom, that's what you have to do.

Q: You have talked about turning poisons into wisdom. Could you explain a bit more about the process?

A: Well, if you look into, say, for example anger. If you are a very angry person, instead of thinking that you have to somehow fight your mind to get rid of this anger, you should use the right method: kindness. Whenever anger comes, you remember the kindness; you summon the kindness. After some time, one day, anger no longer exists because anger causes your kindness to arise. Anger reminds you of kindness. If there were no anger, why should we need kindness? It's there because we need to bring it into action. You can apply the same method with all the other poisons.

According to Tibetan Buddhism, in this training of our mind, our enemy is our best teacher. First, their presence always reminds us of our own poisons. It keeps on showing them, flashing all the time in front of us. Secondly, if we are able to have a proper understanding of the situation and develop loving kindness, our worst enemy helps us to solve our biggest problems.

Usually, we consider whoever is similar to us as our friend. We get along with people because they have similar habits and we don't want to change. So people who like to gossip will come together. Someone who doesn't gossip can't be part of their group. Habits and similarities are very much linked to the kind of people we feel attracted to. But if we always stay with people who have the same qualities and defects as we have, we can't really make much progress because we don't have to question what we are, we are not challenged by something different.

On the contrary, if we're able to move towards our enemy, then it really reminds us of our weaknesses. Someone who has no sympathy for us is showing us what's wrong with us. If you're a good learner, it's like having a teacher there all the time. Your enemy is a very good teacher, constantly telling you what's wrong with you and, if you're wise enough, then you'll make the change.

Q: Lama Yeshe, you talk about getting to the root of the poisons. How do you do that? Is that associated with grasping a thought or is it even before that? Could you also explain the difference between suppression and control of the emotion, anger for instance.

A: First you need to pinpoint your main poison, then use your meditation and knowledge to transform it. Then you can deal with it. The first method to apply is control of the emotion. It's the easiest. It's like you have an electric switch: whenever you see your anger coming, you remember to switch off. This requires awareness. But that's only a temporary solution. In order to find a long-term solution, you need to see why you're angry. Through this investigation, you will be able to deal with it.

In the beginning, you try to control the anger. Whenever you feel very upset, you stop yourself saying things that might hurt other people. If you say nothing, you will not hurt others but you may feel resentment inside. It's a step in the right direction but it's not good enough.

The next step is to see why you are angry, why you got hurt, how you can overcome this chain reaction. You will find out that in most cases, it has to do with attachment and desire. An ordinary person you don't care for can't hurt you so much or make you angry all the time. Those who hurt you most are those you care for, those you are close to and from whom you expect so much. And when you don't get what you think you deserve, then anger starts burning like a volcano. Then you will think, 'Oh, this is what Lama Yeshe has been talking about: attachment. It must be the desire that causes this burning!'

If you are a Vajrayana practitioner, you can then apply the proper practice to overcome attachment and desire, and root out the anger. Vajrayana says that it's a wrong approach to look at everything as 'poisons' we have to get rid of. According to the Vajrayana, the right view would be to see everything as positive, as wisdom, as a source of knowledge. Vajrayana says we don't have to get rid of anything, we have to make it part of us. If you want to make a big, big bonfire, it's better to have as much wood and fuel as you can to make it burn. If there is no fuel, there won't be any fire. This is why Vajrayana is always very challenging, never afraid of anything. With Vajrayana we are always willing to use whatever comes our way to our advantage.

Q: How can I help other people deal with their anger?

A: That's very difficult. I sometimes think that nowadays everybody wants to teach everybody else except themselves. To be able to deal with other people's anger, they have to come to you and ask, 'Please help me to overcome my anger.' This connects the switch. But if you go to them and lecture them, 'You're an angry person, I'm going to sort it out!', you will simply succeed in making them more angry.

We have to stop thinking that we can change other people. First, we should try to help ourselves. I found out that people naturally come to a person who is really free from anger. They talk with that person and gradually they benefit. We can't help someone unless they are asking for help. Help, and especially spiritual help, can never reach anybody unless they open up their door to you. Even

Lamas can't help someone who's angry and doesn't want to be helped. Even if he's my relative, I can't help someone if he doesn't want to be helped. The Buddha himself couldn't help his own cousin, who was very negative. We first need to see whether they're asking for our help. When the wish to be helped is there, then the connection takes place.

Q: If their anger is directed at me, how should I deal with them as a result?

A: You should give them a lot of kindness and think, 'Oh, this must be why we have to use loving kindness.' Just think, 'OK, I can't do anything, because this person is naturally very angry, but as I'm supposed to be practising Buddhism, I should be the one who uses the right methods.' Then mentally develop kindness and a loving attitude towards that person and think how you may one day be able to help. If you're not returning that person's anger, it may put an end to it, because he or she gets no feedback.

It can also be very useful to remember that if there was no anger, we wouldn't have any opportunity to show our kindness. Loving kindness is the key to enlightenment.

However, as I always say, wisdom is necessary. If for instance you have a very abusive partner who has no wisdom, if no matter how much you give in they keep on abusing you all the time, then it's fruitless to show tolerance. If he or she is beating you up every day, if you can't change your partner, giving in is not going to benefit anybody. You don't have to accept this. You can ask yourself: 'Why am I taking all this abuse?' Actually it could be your fault. It's because you have a strong attachment. If you had no attachment, no desire, why would you need to take even one day of such treatment? That's where you have to use wisdom!

Why should you stay together and do nothing but fight? You have not come into this world to fight. This life is about sharing, taking and giving. We call a wise person or a true Buddhist someone who is taking and giving. In a family, it means that both partners bend a little bit towards each other. This is wonderful. Every side is giving a little bit to reach in the middle. But if your partner is always bossing you around and you always have to submit, why do you let such a situation happen? That's because of your own inner poisons, because of your attachment. Suppose you didn't feel attachment and desire for your partner, the minute he or she gave you a hard time, you would say goodbye, enough is enough!

Sometimes some people are so good at making you do the things they want. Having said, 'You're supposed to be a Buddhist, you're supposed to be showing tolerance, loving kindness and compassion!', they feel authorised to treat you like a doormat on which they can wipe their dirty feet! But if you have understood that much, then ask your partner why he or she never wants to be the mat. Isn't that so? Being tolerant means bending on both sides, it means there is giving and taking on both sides. Being free means you are able to change and free yourself from whoever is abusing you. Ongoing arguments and continuous fighting are useless.

Generally, if you have to deal with a really angry human being outside of your family, it's useless to have an argument. They are not part of your life. If showing kindness and understanding helps this person, by all means do so. If not, using skill or wisdom may mean running away! It's very easy. If you know that someone's waiting for you everyday at the corner of the same street, you take another street! It's no big problem. You don't have to confront this person all the time. There's no need to think that you can't run away because you should somehow 'confront your problem.' That's asking for it, isn't it? All we want is to give our mind some calm, some relief from stress. We have ongoing fighting in our head twenty four hours a day, so why should we have to look for more challenges? We really need to use our wisdom.

Of course, if someone can be taught, tamed with loving kindness, then that's what you have to do because, in a way, monsters are monsters because they never had loving kindness. If they're very angry and you react with anger, they'll like it. They're actually feeding on anger. When you show anger, when you fight, that's what they're looking for. It's what they want, how they survive, how they enjoy their life. But as monsters don't know what loving kindness is, if you decide to give them love and kindness, they will stop bothering you! Therefore loving kindness is the right method.

Even the great Milarepa, when he was afflicted by vicious demons, as long as he tried to subdue them, things would only get worse and worse, but when he showed them loving kindness, they dissolved. Monsters are monsters because they don't have wisdom. They just have a head full of poisons, so don't feed them with more negative energy. Don't help small monsters to become big ones!

We should instead try to visualise the angry person as an ice-cube and visualize ourselves as the sun, feeling that the sun of our loving kindness is melting his or her anger. The antidote to all anger-related poisons is loving-kindness.

Sometimes it is difficult for us to feel loving kindness towards people who behave very badly, with lots of cruelty. Such as when we see human beings slaughtering each other in some parts of the world, sometimes even singing songs and seemingly enjoying it, or when we see them slaughtering animals - some clever people say that animals don't have feelings, how do they know they have no feelings? What we are currently doing to animals is totally unacceptable!

In order to feel compassion for these beings who act so wrongly, we should again develop our wisdom and understand that the cause of their cruel behaviour is precisely a lack of wisdom. Let's take the case of parents mistreating their children. If they were leading a peaceful, stable, decent life, they would never abuse their children. Nobody deliberately, knowingly, happily, hurts others. Look at the animal world: even they are willing to give their lives to protect their offspring. Some human beings are leading such miserable lives or have themselves experienced so much abuse and suffering that they don't know how to be kind and loving. Instead, whenever they are angry, they abuse their children. They don't know how to behave differently, how to control themselves. If we really carefully consider their situation, we should feel deeply sorry for them instead of getting angry. They have been through such difficult times that even when they want to do their very best, they lack the wisdom and ability to be loving and caring.

Those parents suffered exactly like their children do now. They have unknowingly carried this family lineage of suffering on to their children. But it is now up to the children to stop this suffering lineage by understanding that nobody ever intentionally wanted to hurt them. They can decide to stop this pain and be free. We should all have developed some wisdom by now and realise that we should not follow certain destructive traditions that have so far been passed from one generation to the next. We should not have a loyalty towards traditions that are not beneficial for us and are actually capable of taking away from us what is most important, namely our inner peace and our physical health.

Q: Is the idea of attachment in children different from that in adults? Because for adults, you talk about relationships and about not being attached, but for children, attachment is very, very important. It seems to me that it helps them to feel secure.

A: It is indeed quite different, because until it grows up a child completely depends on you. You are responsible for your child, you're part of its life. So if a child builds up more attachment, maybe he simultaneously builds up more confidence in your ability to look after and guide him, so I can't say there's anything wrong with this form of natural bond.

Q: Could you please give some advice about finding a balance between providing for your children materially, spending time with them and also having time for yourself?
A: You should find a middle path! You need to earn enough so that you can really take good care of them. And you can give your children good quality time. When you

spend, say, four hours of your precious time with your daughter, be a very good, very kind mother. And when you're working, concentrate on your job. It's no use to stay together with your child twenty four hours and then beat her up!

Q: When I am focusing on an object and I just look at this object, I see many things in it. Does that mean that my mind is not still yet?

A: Definitely. You won't be able to focus your vision on one object all straight away. You need to train in it. To see an object, the only thing we have are our eyes and it keeps us busy.

But if you're a beginner, then you will get involved with all the details, the individual characteristics, you will single things out and be completely carried away by all these things. This means that you are mentally creating your own chaos by analyzing. A true meditator, will not become too involved with the object if that starts to happen, just rest and relax. Meditation is a gradual, gradual training.

Q: You said that in meditation the mind wanders and we should bring it back to the object. When I do this, the meditation session becomes very stressful and full of conflict. There is conflict between the mind wandering and me trying to stop it wandering.

A: Yes, that's true, not only stressful, but you become very tense. What happens is that usually your mind is all over the place, scattered everywhere. Now that you are trying to discipline it for the first time, it doesn't like it. That's why what I'm teaching you here are actually methods that you can apply for your whole life. If you can practise the three types of meditation that I have given you, you will be a better meditator.

Firstly, when you have energy, you can make some effort and use the 'one pointedness' meditation, focusing on an object and bringing the mind back. It's like you're really getting down to it. Your mind was scattered everywhere, now you're bringing it into oneness.

Secondly, once you have achieved this, then your greatest obstacle will be your doubts. You can then use the method of investigation. Instead of wondering, 'Is what the Lama teaches true? Is religion true? Is the book true?', you can, through this investigation, during meditation, find the answers by yourself. You can free yourself from doubts.

And thirdly, when you feel too uptight, the antidote to free this tension is to relax, to ask your mind nothing. Just let go.

You can use this combination of techniques over many days or during one and the same session. Whatever your problem, you apply the right method. When you're very uptight and tense, you relax. When your mind is all over the place, you bring it back to oneness and in order to achieve this, you need to focus on something. And when you feel uneasy about what you're doing, when you sit thinking, 'Oh, maybe I don't really believe in what I'm doing, is it really true or not true?', then you start investigating.

For Mahamudra practitioners, the greatest obstacle is doubt. Doubt is actually the only obstacle, because Mahamudra is all about knowing, deep down in our mind, that our Buddha nature is pure and perfect. It's about feeling very confident that we don't need to use any method or form, that there is nothing we need to do because it's all perfect as it is. This is why we want to be free from doubts. Therefore, for me, these three different methods are actually all we need and all we'll ever need.

Q: I feel I need to engage in everyday life in order to face my anger. How does one deal with anger?

A: You may think you are dealing with these things and that you are confronting them, but at the same time, you're already harming someone else. There has to be another party. It may be that you are aggressive and feel you need someone to confront. It seems to you that you're feeling better after the clash, but at the same time, you've hurt another person.

    The Buddhist approach is not to confront another being, but to confront ourselves. So if I have a big, big anger, instead of thinking I have to be angry with somebody, shouting or kicking, I try to see what causes my anger. I need to see how to deal with my anger. In that way, I will be able to completely root out all the anger and, at the same time, not give any problem to anybody else. I think that's the proper way of dealing with negative emotions.

Q: During meditation, should we breathe through the mouth or through the nostrils?
A: It really doesn't matter. Mahamudra people say one should breathe through the nose, but in the Dzogchen tradition for instance, they just breathe in and out through the mouth, gazing into space and totally opening up. Whichever suits you is right for you. Whatever is natural to you is the best. Don't worry too much about this.

Q: When breathing in four phases (breathing in, holding the breath, breathing out, making a pause before starting again), I experience a kind of torpor. I feel like yawning and tears start coming, and during the whole session, it doesn't stop.

A: Traditionally, we say that breathing meditation is useful because we don't need to 'do' anything. We should just breathe normally, as we usually do, without adding or changing anything. So if you can be relaxed and more natural, it will be good.

Many of you have experience in trying out other people's cultures and traditions. People sometimes visualise prana, nadi and chakra and many teachers are also very happy to give you such techniques. There are methods where you try to hold your breath and play with prana and nadi, but I found out that in the West, most people have lots of wind energy and, according to my understanding and experience, trying to use these subtle energies sometimes brings lots of mental obstacles and is often more harmful to you than beneficial. That is why I do not try to teach these techniques. Some people who are very heavy, very solid, who are not sort of woken up, then for them, using this prana and nadi could be very useful. Otherwise, for the majority of people, I can see a lot of problems. Prana, nadi and chakra are very sensitive and if your mind is chaotic, triggering them creates more emotions, more problems.

In your case, and for others with the same problem, you can use the following method: you put a small pebble, a little stone in front of you and you focus on it. Don't examine the size, the colour or the shape but just focus your mind on the object. That is called in Mahamudra 'focusing the mind on an impure object'.

Our mind is like a wild, untamed horse. Our awareness, our remembrance, is like a lasso. We throw the rope around the horse and this object we are focussing on is like a pole. But if the rope is very tight, we can't tame the horse, the horse gets even wilder. We should give him plenty of rope to go around, but not totally let him run away. The method is just to focus gently, without analysing, without researching, just leaving things alone. It is also a very good method.

Q: When I meditate, can I look at a picture of a Lama or visualize him instead of focusing on an object? If one has had a good connection with a teacher, is it good to think of him, imagine that one is receiving his blessings, even if he is dead?

A: In all four major Tibetan schools, it is said that if one has a Lama or a teacher whom one can trust, in whom one feels great faith, the very best method is to visualise him and receive his blessings. If you have such a person, you are very fortunate.

Q: Should I recite the Refuge and develop Bodhicitta each time before the meditation?
A: Refuge is very important, Bodhicitta is very important, and both won't take much time. So recite both!
Q: Could you give us advice as to how much time to spend on studies and how much on meditation?

A: A bird needs two wings to fly. If you accumulate all the information and are not able to actually put it into practice, that is not going to change you. At the same time, if you don't know what to do in the meditation, you can't progress. You cannot meditate in the darkness of not knowing what to do, but I cannot think of anybody gaining a profound inner spiritual realisation without meditation. All the saints, all the historically great precious teachers - and this is also true for Christianity - were meditators. I haven't heard of Milarepa studying at great length, yet he attained Buddhahood in one lifetime through diligent meditation. The Buddha himself obtained enlightenment through many lifetimes of accumulating knowledge and through meditating. It suits European minds very well to do physical activities and engage mentally, whereas you find it more or less impossible to meditate because your mind doesn't know what to do! That is why there are less and less meditators, and more and more people who study. The end result is that many people become disillusioned!

Q: If we start the day with a meditation session, how can we maintain this meditative state of mind throughout the day?

A: Awareness! Awareness! Awareness! But you can only achieve it if you start with at least twenty minutes of meditation every morning and tell yourself that you want to be aware of everything that happens through the day. Then you try to maintain this idea all the way through. When you drive, you know you are driving. When doing your job, you know you are doing your job. You keep the awareness alive, which means that you remember what you have to remember.

Q: To meditate properly, do we need to generate devotion and compassion or can we just leave the mind as it is?

A: According to Gampopa's teachings, meditation is everything. It is purification as well as accumulation of merit

142

and wisdom, and it covers all the practices that we normally do. If you are able to meditate, you are doing everything

Devotion can only come when we have self-confidence. If we have no confidence and feel unhappy, learning to trust is difficult. First you have to be able to trust, as devotion is above trust. You just keep on meditating. Developing Bodhicitta mind is like planting seeds of loving kindness.

You should always start with a devotional prayer, saying that if you cannot achieve your aspiration by yourself, if your mind poisons and negativities are too strong, then you need to achieve it through blessings. Devotional prayers are very powerful. You wholeheartedly pray for help. Out of their compassion, Bodhisattvas like Chenrezig or Tara can manifest in our mind, like rainbows in the sky, whenever we need them. As long as we have this solid, dualistic mind, we are only able to practise when we feel there is something external to relate to and receive blessings from. Praying for blessings is like throwing seeds in the field of our mind. Gradually, devotion will start to grow, because the practice changes our situation. Dharma is actually giving us greater confidence and also helping us to improve. When we see that our practice brings results, we develop greater confidence in the teachings and the teachers, and this naturally gives rise to devotion.

LOOKING TO THE FUTURE...

At present Lama Yeshe Losal is very much involved in various projects which reflect his wish to establish the Dharma in the West. As Abbot of Karma Drupgyud Darjay Ling Monastery at Samye Ling in Scotland, much of his time and energy is spent overseeing the building of Samye Project Phase II. This second phase consists of two wings that will adjoin the existing temple to provide monastic accommodation, apartments for visiting lamas, dining hall and kitchen facilities, Tibetan and English libraries, a conference room and an audio/visual studio.

In recent years Lama Yeshe has become well known for his involvement with interdenominational activities both at home and abroad. He takes every opportunity to develop harmony and good communications within the Buddhist community and has many friends within the Theravadin and Zen traditions. He also works closely with the Scottish Interfaith Council and has been asked by the high profile Buddhist-Christian Conference to host their 2003 meeting at Samye Ling, which has provided an added impetus for the speedy completion of Samye Project Phase II. The outer structure of the first wing has been completed and work will continue to fit and furnish the interior, as funds become available. The monks and nuns to be housed within Samye Phase II will all have life-long vows and will form the nucleus of Lama Yeshe's Sangha.

For Buddhism to be firmly rooted in the West, Lama Yeshe feels it is essential to have a strong and committed Sangha. Allied to this aspiration was the establishment of the Samye Sangha Foundation that Lama Yeshe founded in 1995 with a view providing for the ordained monks and nuns. Although it is still in its infancy, the aim of the Foundation is to become a self-sufficient organisation, run by Sangha members themselves, and supported by the wider community. It is dedicated to enabling the monks and nuns of Samye Ling to pursue their spiritual path for the benefit of all beings.

Another important way to fully establish the Dharma in order to bring inner peace and happiness to our culture is through the practice of meditation. In his role as Retreat Master, Lama Yeshe is responsible for separate retreat centres for men and women. A growing number of lay people, as well as monks and nuns take part in these retreats - varying in length from just a few days to one year or more - under Lama Yeshe's direction.

The traditional practice of three year three month retreats, which give dedicated practitioners the opportunity to fully engage in spiritual life, are set to begin again in 2002. The men's retreat will take place at a farmhouse on the Isle of Arran known as Samye Dechen Ling, which is currently being converted to accommodate twenty-one men. Meanwhile the women's retreat, scheduled to begin in autumn 2002, will take place on Holy Island in the lighthouse cottages at the south end of the island which have been specially converted for the purpose. Later, as funding becomes available, Lama Yeshe intends that further long retreats will be held in the new Retreat Centre that will be built according to an environmentally friendly and innovative award winning design

Meanwhile, the Centre for World Peace and Health is under construction at the north end of the island. This will house up to fifty people and provide conference facilities for one hundred. It is Lama Yeshe's hope that this unique resource will be used for regular inter-faith dialogue as well as by people of different beliefs and health oriented groups wishing to hold courses and workshops. Thanks to Lama Yeshe's inspiring vision and tireless energy the Holy Island Project has already built up a worldwide reputation. Working with environmental experts will ensure that all building development is carried out with minimum impact on the island's unique ecology.

Lama Yeshe's plans for Holy Island arise from the Buddhist perspective of respecting every spring, tree and rock so that Holy Island will become the holiest of places where people can gain inner wisdom. The combination of pure minds within a pure environment will be of great benefit and inspiration to people everywhere. As Lama Yeshe Losal himself says, 'One day, Holy Island will be home to many Dharma practitioners who will dedicate their lives to achieving realisation, or Buddhahood, for the benefit of all sentient beings. Once we have attained that, then Buddhism will truly become a part of western civilisation and culture. My prayer is that, before I die, there will be many realised beings on Holy Island.'

If you wish to know more about any of the projects mentioned above, please contact the appropriate office, as listed below, at the Samye Ling address or check out the relevant web-site.

Samye Project Phase II
tel. 013873 73232 Ext 3
email scotland@samyeling.org
www.samyeling.org

Samye Sangha Foundation
tel. 013873 73232 Ext 27
email scotland@samyeling.org
www.samyeling.org

Holy Island Project
tel.013873 73232 Ext 2
email office@holyisland.org
www.holyisland.org

The Sangha proceeding from Samye Ling temple.

Lama Yeshe Losal leads practioners out of the long retreat and into Samye Ling.

Samye Ling Stupa - Winter 2001.

Photo Rinchen Khandro

Lama Yeshe Losal on the ferry to Holy Island.

Photo Murdo MacLeod

Lama Yeshe Losal with the Sangha on Holy Island.

Lama Yeshe Losal with the White Tara rock painting on Holy Island